When God Becomes Goddess

When God Becomes Goddess

The Transformation
of American Religion

RICHARD GRIGG

CONTINUUM • NEW YORK

1995
The Continuum Publishing Company
370 Lexington Avenue
New York, NY 10017

Printed in the United States of America

Library of Congress Cataloging-in-Publication Data

Grigg, Richard, 1955–
    When God becomes goddess : the transformation of American religion / Richard Grigg.
        p.   cm.
    Includes bibliographical references and index.
    ISBN 0-8264-0864-8 (hardcover : alk. paper)
    1. God—History of doctrines—20th century.   2. Christianity—United States—History—20th century.   3. Feminist theology.
    4. Goddess religion.   I. Title.
    BT102.G747   1995
    231'.0973'0904—dc20   95-20444
                                                                        CIP

Portions of Chapter III originally appeared in "Enacting the Divine: Feminist Theology and the Being of God," in *The Journal of Religion* 74 (October 1994): 506–23, copyright 1994, the University of Chicago. The author gratefully acknowledges the permission of the University of Chicago to reprint this material.

For

Hannah Marie Grigg

Contents

Introduction

$\mathcal{F}$or over a century, the disciples of Nietzsche's madman have echoed his claim that God is dead. But the prophet of the death of God neglected to say anything about the Goddess, and this oversight provides a metaphorical starting point for the argument pursued in this book. The traditional Western notion of deity may be destined not for obliteration but, rather, for transformation. Perhaps God will not simply disappear, but will in some fashion become Goddess.

In order to evaluate this possibility, we must first consider whether it is in fact the case that the traditional concept of God is no longer viable. It is a truism in some philosophical and even theological circles that the traditional God, who is conceived as a supernatural personal agent or supreme being, is unthinkable now. No one should be surprised to find that a book published in the early 1970s, coming as it did on the heels of "death of God" theology, asserts that "belief in God has disappeared, at least as an effective element of contemporary living."[1] But even a much more recent book claims that "Our symbol of 'God,' heavy with the mythic overtones of our religious traditions, suggests a kind of being—an all-powerful sovereign, creator, and king of the universe—which no longer seems intelligible in our world, and which, moreover, may today deeply offend our moral sensibilities."[2]

At least from the vantage point of contemporary American consciousness, there is something terribly odd about these confident
remarks. A significant portion of the U.S. population appears to have
no inkling of the death of the traditional God. Survey after survey
indicates that God is firmly ensconced in the belief systems of the
American populace. Belief in God is impossible, it seems, only for an
isolated group of intellectuals.

Yet I do not wish to imply that all of the obituaries for God are
thoroughly misguided. On the contrary, the traditional God is indeed
doomed, but I shall argue that this is not because it is now impossible
to believe in him. Instead, belief in the traditional God has taken on a
wholly new meaning in the context of contemporary first-world culture, and this new meaning is at odds with what is essential to the
very notion of deity. Namely, the traditional notion of God is privatized, inevitably so, in the contemporary context. Thus, the demise of
the God of traditional theism turns out to be a more subtle affair than
is often realized.

At the same time, this demise may also turn out to be more
decisive than the death of God as ordinarily conceived, for from this
perspective it appears to make no difference how many persons still
exercise belief in the traditional God or how strongly they do so:
belief in such a God simply no longer signifies what it once did.

To say that God becomes Goddess is a way of suggesting that
the demise of the God of traditional theism is not the end of the
notion of deity altogether, but that the essential burden of that
notion, which can no longer be borne by traditional theism, is taken
up by a new concept of the divine. Some of the trappings of our concept of God change, in other words, so that the essential core can be
preserved. This is a matter of continuity in change, of transformation
rather than of simple dissolution.

I have no intention of suggesting in what follows that this transformation is predetermined; my argument is not that the idea of God
will necessarily be transformed in one particular way. Rather, I want
to argue that the basic Western notion of deity is ripe for transformation, and that we see one form of transformation in a current of contemporary feminist religious thought. The argument of this book

should be taken as an attempt to test the transformation hypothesis by following only one of the several avenues to transformation that may exist.

In exploring the transformation of God into Goddess, it is important to keep both the element of continuity and the element of change clearly in view. Much of the most interesting feminist religious thought appears to present a view of the divine radically different from what has been meant by God in the Jewish and Christian religious traditions. It is of course necessary for feminist theologians to emphasize the changes, in order to free themselves from what they regard as the destructive patriarchal elements of Jewish and Christian God-talk. But I wish to put a good deal of emphasis on the continuities that also exist here. In fact, I shall argue that a feminist reconstruction of the divine is able to preserve the essence of the Western notion of God, while, paradoxically, more traditional ways of thinking about God no longer express that essence. We ought to remember that feminist theology, however much it may reach back to sources outside Judaism and Christianity, is still the product of a cultural environment that has been formed by Jewish and Christian sensibilities about the divine. We can never leap entirely out of our cultural world and the grammar of meaning that it provides. Indeed, one might well argue, for example, that the impulse toward sociopolitical liberation that animates much of feminist religious thought is recognizably Hebraic in origin. It should not be surprising, then, that there are elements of continuity hidden beneath the differences that characterize the relation between the Jewish and Christian God, on the one hand, and the contemporary feminists' Goddess, on the other.

If these observations are intended to allay the anxieties of feminist thinkers about having their ideas of Goddess too closely tied to the traditional Western concept of the divine, the anxieties of those who wish to defend traditional Judaism and Christianity must also be addressed. One can imagine a Jewish thinker saying, for example, that this project of seeing some continuity between the Jewish approach to God and the general Western notion of deity, and from there to contemporary feminist discussions of Goddess must inevitably fail: the Jewish notion of God is not part of some more general theological dynamic; it is inherently specific, for this God is the God of a particular history, and he is the God of the Torah. Similarly, a Christian thinker is apt to say that the Christian idea of God is in no way a function of some larger tradition of reflection, for the Christian God is always and only the God concretely revealed in the life, death, and resurrection of Jesus Christ. But, particularly in the Christian case, these objections are not wholly convincing. First of all, the Christian concept of God is dependent upon Jewish piety. However central the Christ may be for a Christian understanding of the nature of God, Christian interpretations of the Christ were initially worked out within the context of the Jewish tradition and its teaching about God. The gracious God of Christianity is recognizable as the same God whose *hesed*, or "loving-kindness," is celebrated in the Hebrew Bible. Furthermore, Christian theology has clearly imbibed other currents in the ongoing formulation of its concept of God, most notably various tenets of Greek philosophy, as critics of the Hellenization of Christian thought never tire of pointing out.

Those determined to protect the specific characteristics of the Jewish or Christian God should also consider the possibility that some of those specific characteristics have in fact been taken up in something as apparently foreign as feminist talk about the Goddess. The Goddess is usually depicted by feminists as the benevolent source of life that empowers women and can vouchsafe them a sense of dignity and possibility. As such, she probably has more in common with the God of Judaism and Christianity than with many an ancient divinity. In the pages that follow, I sometimes refer to the transformed divinity that emerges from feminist thought as "God"—she preserves the essence of the God of traditional Western religious consciousness—but I more often designate her "Goddess," both to emphasize the changes that constitute the transformation process and to be true to the intentions of (at least some of) the feminist thinkers upon whom I draw. I refer to the God of traditional theism with the pronoun "he" throughout my discussion. This is the common practice within traditional theism itself, of course, and it helps to distinguish the God of traditional theism from the transformed version of divinity, for which I use the pronoun "she."

Chapter I sets the stage for the argument that follows by discussing the ambiguous state of religion in contemporary American culture. The ambiguity can be taken as a clue to the fact that religion is undergoing a transformation.

Chapter II argues that the meaning of traditional theistic assertions are changed by what I term the peculiarly contemporary form of the problem of theodicy. The existence of evil and suffering has been a perennial difficulty for those who believe in a benevolent supreme being. But a qualitatively different form of the problem of theodicy appears in the contemporary First World. Our communication technologies confront us with so many instances of human suffering from so many places that it is no longer possible to find the kind of meaningful pattern that any successful theodicy demands. Furthermore, other instances of technology, especially medical technology, allow human beings themselves to alleviate suffering in a way that leads us to question why God could not have done so long ago.

These difficulties do not render belief in God as a supernatural personal agent immediately incoherent or impossible. On the contrary, many intelligent and sensitive persons continue to embrace this concept of God. But in order to do so, they must unconsciously restrict God's reach to the private sphere; they do not envision God as a determinative influence in the realms of nature and history where the contemporary form of the problem of theodicy arises. As a result, the import of belief in God is radically changed. Traditional theism's concept of God is employed in a way that destroys the meaning of traditional theism; its God dies while apparently being affirmed by a host of devotees.

It is in Chapter III that we come to the actual transformation of God. I shall attempt to show how a current of feminist religious thought accomplishes this transformation by implicitly conceiving of God as a relation that is enacted by human beings, in conjunction with nature and the power of being. Chapters IV and V deal with some of the implications and results of this radical transformation of the sacred, both positive and negative. In the Epilogue, I return briefly to theodicy, and consider just how the transformed deity fares when confronted with that issue.

I talked with many people while writing this book. Some of them will find little here with which they can agree. But I am grateful for the conversations that I have shared with them, whether those conversations bore directly or indirectly on this project. I have had numerous discussions on women and religion with Serinity Young and Jennifer Rycenga. And I always look forward to lunch conversations with my departmental colleagues Walter Brooks and John Berkman. I owe special thanks to those who commented on a draft of the manuscript: Dennis Bielfeldt, Walter Brooks, Steve Gowler, and Michael Raposa. Finally, many thanks to Cynthia Eller of Continuum. The book has benefited from her impressive abilities as both an editor and a scholar of religion.

❧ I ❧

Has Religion Been Reborn?

T he Enlightenment promised to undo religion. At the very least, the Enlightenment mindset attempted to remove the miraculous, the dogmatic, and the merely traditional from religion, thus reducing it to a function of reason. This "religion within the limits of reason alone" might well lead to the Jesus of Thomas Jefferson's aggressively abridged New Testament: a wise moral teacher with no more claim to divinity than any other human being.[1] Perhaps even as late as the 1960s one could have believed that this Enlightenment dynamic was still working itself out, however circuitously. After all, a theological movement burst upon the scene in Britain and the United States announcing the advent of a "religionless Christianity," a Christianity that turned away from God and toward a Jesus bearing a surprising resemblance to the one described by Jefferson.[2] Needless to say, the majority of Christians did not embrace this radical reduction of Christian belief. But a contemporary advocate of the Enlightenment might point out that despite the apparent failure of proposals for a religionless Christianity, much of twentieth-century Christianity, mainline Protestantism in particular, does appear doctrinally spartan when compared to premodern forms of the faith. Reform Judaism is roughly analogous to mainline Protestantism in this regard. If the Enlightenment goal has not been attained, one could nevertheless argue that history is still moving in that direction.

In addition to this whittling away of its traditional theological substance, religion's structural relation to Western society seems to have become ever more tenuous as time has gone by. While the Christian religion once stood as the unifying center of Western society, the period stretching from the seventeenth century all the way into the twentieth has seen religion's larger social authority continually diminish. This privatization of religion is an essential element in what has come to be known as secularization. Present-day champions of the Enlightenment could claim that the religious reductionism entailed by privatization is at least consistent with the most severe Enlightenment predictions, and possibly that this is but an evolutionary step on the way to ever more reductive assaults upon the substance of religion.

Of course this picture is much too simple. In the United States, in particular, there have always been signs of religious vitality alongside the signs of religious decline. But especially in the last few decades of the twentieth century, the Enlightenment certainty of religion's demise, or of its distillation into a product of pure reason, has become almost laughable. In fact, we suddenly find ourselves witnessing what appears to be a resurgence of religion.

The signs of this renewed religious vitality are many. To begin with, numerous polls suggest that Americans currently believe in God, angels, and the afterlife in surprising numbers, and that they are faithfully attending churches and synagogues.[3] And despite the dynamic of privatization that the Enlightenment and other modern historical forces have visited upon religion, Americans are paying increased attention to the relation of religion to public life. This is nowhere more evident than in the involvement of religious groups in the debate about abortion. In a similar vein, the government's heretofore absolute prohibition of prayer and religion in the public schools is being tested and retested in court cases and public debates around the nation.[4] And while the world of scholarship has, in general, paid little serious attention to religion during much of this century, here too one finds a new interest in religion and its role in society. Witness the heading of a lengthy article in *The Chronicle of Higher Education*: "Growing number of researchers investigate the role of the spiritual in people's lives."[5] Indeed, "from mystical experiences to church bazaars," reports the *Chronicle*, "researchers are tracking the impact of religion on society."[6] Even sectors of American culture that have in the past been not just indifferent but openly hostile to religion are, in some cases, rethinking their position. The American Psychiatric Association, for instance, has updated its *Diagnostic and Statistical Manual of Mental Disorders* so as to suggest that, contrary to past perceptions, religious and spiritual problems need not automatically be considered signs of mental illness.[7]

To these individual indicators of religious vitality one must add a consideration of general social currents that tend to reinforce an appreciation of religion. It has become the common wisdom that we live in the postmodern era, and postmodernism—as self-conscious opposition to modernity[8]—consists, in large part, of disdain for the Enlightenment and all it valued. Hence, the narrow and overconfident rationalism that promised the end of religion is now itself out of fashion. Some even take this as the beginning of a "New Age" in which, apparently, every whim of the religious imagination can be indulged.

We ought not overlook multiculturalism either, for this movement too has a part to play in the renewed interest in religion in American society. Multiculturalism encourages Americans to look beyond the majority culture, the animating spirit of which owes so much to the Enlightenment and modernity, and to look appreciatively at cultural traditions in which religion typically plays a more central role. African-American and Hispanic cultural traditions, for example, clearly have profound religious dimensions. To look beyond the majority culture in American society is also to note the powerful role of religion in other parts of the world, from post-Communist Russia and the former Soviet Republics to the Mideast.

Who could blame an advocate of religion, then, for displaying an exhuberant optimism about the future of religion in American culture? Perhaps we are on the verge of another Great Awakening. But this picture is also too simplistic. Just as the Enlightenment expectation of religion's demise or reduction was naive and hasty, so the assumption that secularization has been halted and religion reborn is suspect, especially given the significant counterevidence.

First, while the newspapers are indeed full of stories suggesting the influence of religion in the contemporary world, much of the news is bad. A large part of the animus behind the attack that the Christian Serbs mounted on their Muslim neighbors in the former Yugoslavia had to do precisely with the fact of those neighbors being Muslim. The Serbs feared, so they said, the creation of a Muslim state in Eastern Europe.[9] There has been continual violence between Hindus and Muslims in India, as well as violence instigated by Sikhs. Protestants and Catholics have killed each other in Northern Ireland for decades. In Switzerland, over forty members of a religious group known as the Solar Temple were found dead, apparently victims of intrasect murder and of suicide. And in this country, the most spectacular news about religion in the last quarter of the century includes the mass death of Jim Jones' followers, the fiery end of messianic pretender David Koresh and his Branch Davidian disciples, the sexual and monetary escapades of television evangelists, and the widespread allegations of sexual abuse leveled against the Roman Catholic clergy.

Second, it is frequently observed that the most vital segment of American religion is a conservative version of Christianity variously labeled "fundamentalism," "evangelical Christianity," or the "Christian right." It is the conservative churches whose membership rolls are growing, and it is their preachers who dominate the Sunday morning airwaves with their high-tech television ministries. The most vigorous religious groups in other parts of the world are also, in many cases, fundamentalist in their orientation, with Muslim fundamentalism the most familiar and politically significant example. Whatever their strengths, these groups represent a ghettoized religiosity, one that is comfortable writing off other groups and world views. Of course the Medieval church already declared that salvation was not a possibility outside its walls, but the nature of Medieval Europe precluded the kind of religious pluralism that characterizes the contemporary world; the Jews, for example, were a persecuted minority rather than neighbors who represented an alternative to Christianity. But today's fundamentalists, especially in the United States, live in the midst of an unavoidable religious pluralism, and they draw upon it in order to define themselves: part of their zeal appears to be a function of their sense of "us against them," the true believers versus the lost. This ghettoization is only reinforced by certain tendencies within postmodernism—however different a fashionable and intellectual postmodernism may initially seem from right-wing religion. Postmodernism is dismissive of any notion of universal reason, on the basis of which all persons might discuss, argue, and defend their various beliefs. Universal reason is seen as hopelessly modern, a totalizing, totalitarian legacy of the Enlightenment. Thus, postmodernism rejects the possibility of an overarching "metanarrative."[10] Each group, or perhaps even each individual, will be left with its own idiosyncratic story. While this does not count against the bare claim that religion is being reborn—religion can as easily come to life in an unattractive shape as an attractive one—it does suggest that this particular piety is ultimately destructive and thus not conducive to the long-term vitality of religion. Given what we already know about the results of social fragmentation—consider the ethnic violence breaking out around the world and the racial tensions in this country—and given the issues that demand a unified response from the peoples of the world—the ecological crisis, for example—it is difficult to be sanguine about a revival of religion that takes this ghettoized form.

Third, it is not clear that the privatization of religion, which is one of the hallmarks of secularization, is actually being reversed. On the one hand, Americans' religious beliefs must surely inform their political commitments and their visions of social morality. To take but one example, those committed to a conservative religious world view will tend to support capital punishment, while those whose religious sensibilities are more liberal will often oppose it.[11] But, on the other hand, the particular social issues that seem to be of most concern to religious persons and groups, and that receive most attention in the press, are not *only* social: many of them, such as abortion or AIDS or the breakdown of the family, are also firmly tied to the private sphere.

Religion still seems a private phenomenon in our society. Not only are the moral issues it addresses often at least partly private, it is also only morality upon which religion exercises influence. Is there any sense in which religion significantly informs the larger intellectual framework of contemporary society? That task appears to fall much more to science than to religion. While educated persons today are much more realistic about how and what science can know than were the naive and enthusiastic advocates of science in the past (there is even something of a backlash against science and technology in contemporary popular culture), it does not appear that much has changed in the relative social roles of science and religion since the nineteenth century.

The story has often been told about how Napoleon, upon having read the work of the philosopher and mathematician Laplace, remarked on how Laplace tried to understand the universe without reference to God. Laplace is supposed to have replied, "Sir, I have no need of that hypothesis." This is not necessarily an expression of hostility toward God and religion, but simply an indication that God does not do any work in Laplace's intellectual exploration of the world. If we jump to the present day and look at cosmologist Stephen Hawking's surprise bestseller, *A Brief History of Time*, we find the same essential attitude. Hawking actually mentions God fairly frequently, but he cannot seem to find much for God to do.[12] And while contemporary theologians have come up with provocative and even convincing ways to harmonize religion and present-day science, religion contributes little to the *cognitive* framework through which educated Westerners view the world—physics, genetics, and biologically oriented psychiatry do this job.[13]

Furthermore, although there are polls that seem to suggest that Americans are very pious today, startlingly more pious than their European cousins, it has been argued that this unique, quintessentially American form of piety is defined precisely by its radically private, personal character. It is definitive of the "American religion," which Harold Bloom so provocatively describes, to look not to a God who calls us beyond our focus upon the individual self, but to a deity who validates the importance of the solitary soul and recognizes it as in its own way divine.[14]

In their indictment of American individualism in *Habits of the Heart*, Robert Bellah and his colleagues do not spare religion: here too they see a focus on individual and personal concerns that powerfully undermines any attempt to deal with larger social realities. The private character of American piety is probably nowhere more graphically presented than in their account of a young woman named Sheila who has pieced together her own religion, naming it "Sheilaism." As they point out, "'Sheilaism' somehow seems a perfectly natural expression of current American religious life."[15]

There are other, perhaps even more fundamental, questions that ought to be asked about these polls that reassure us that we are as pious, or even more pious, than ever. How much trust should we put in them? A recent study that compared actual church attendance figures with polling data discovered that perhaps only half as many people actually attend church regularly as claim to attend.[16] Consider also the fact that a bare "yes" in response to a pollster's inquiry as to whether one believes in God tells us very little. It provides no clue as to the intensity of the belief or of the role it plays in the respondent's life. And, in fact, if we do decide to put some stock in what the polls say, we can find other polling data that suggests American religiosity is waning, at least by some measures. Sociologist of religion Robert Wuthnow has summarized some of this data as follows:

> In 1952, 75 percent of the American public said religion was very important in their lives; since the 1980s, that figure has been hovering around 55 percent. . . .
>
> In 1957, 81 percent of the American public thought religion provided answers to all or most of today's problems; by 1984, this figure had slipped to 56 percent.
>
> In 1963, 65 percent of the American public said the Bible is the inspired word of God and should be taken literally, word for word; in 1992, only 32 percent of the public gave this response.[17]

What are we to conclude from all of this? Is religion resurgent, or is it still doomed to the fate that its Enlightenment critics envisioned for it? Or do the countervailing pieces of evidence mean that there is no definite trend in the struggle between religion and the various forces arrayed against it, but only an ambiguous back-and-forth? Perhaps none of these possibilities quite fits the bill. Consider another option: maybe religion is neither simply resurgent nor destined to pass away, nor is it caught in a holding action. Perhaps, instead, it is in a process of being transformed. To put it a bit differently, some significant elements of traditional religious belief and practice are passing away, but a new kind of religiosity is poised to take its place. This process of religious transformation is a matter of continuity in change: very real differences emerge when this new religiosity is compared with religion as it was previously understood and practiced, but there is a genuine continuity of what defines Western religion in the midst of these changes. In fact it may be that the changes are necessary, given the changing cultural environment, if the continuity is to exist. This is indeed the claim that I wish to make: that religion is being transformed in contemporary first-world culture; that it is undergoing radical changes that, paradoxically, are required to preserve its identity.

One kind of transformation thesis can be supported by functional definitions of religion, such as those offered by Paul Tillich, a theologian, and Thomas Luckmann, a sociologist. Tillich, in what may be the most famous attempt to define religion in the twentieth century, describes religion as "ultimate concern": whatever functions as the unconditional concern around which all of my other concerns are organized, and which is my key to dealing with the fundamental challenges of human existence, is what deserves the name "religion."[18] At least when we take this component of Tillich's work in isolation from his larger theological and normative interests, we can say that he is not defining religion substantively, in terms of some particular content of belief or practice, but in terms of the role that religion plays in human consciousness.[19] This allows for the possibility that the contents of traditional religion—the teachings of Christian orthodoxy or of classical rabbinic Judaism, for example—may pass from the scene, but that some new ultimate concern will take their place and carry out the same role in people's lives.

In a roughly similar fashion, Luckmann defines religion as the socially objectivated system of meaning persons use to orient their lives. Like Tillich, Luckmann does not focus on some particular content as definitive of religion, but rather on the role religion plays. As a result, he can argue that while there have been vast changes in religious belief and even in the institutional location of religion in modern Western society, religion lives on. Once again we can talk about a basic continuity, specified in terms of function, in the midst of changes in belief and practice.[20]

But it is another kind of transformation and another type of continuity amidst change that I shall propose. To begin with, note that while the decision about what constitutes religion is not arbitrary, neither is it a matter of objective fact. There is no "essence" of religion if the word "essence" be taken in naively ontological terms (i.e., as some unchanging heart of religion that makes it what it is independently of human judgments about it). It is a matter of interpretation what is essential to religion, interpretation carried out precisely in the attempt to define religion. This apparent circularity does not mean that there are no limits or guidelines to determine how one should define religion. Most of all, a definition should be useful, it should accomplish something that the investigator who creates it wishes to accomplish. As Clifford Geertz observes, "although it is notorious that definitions establish nothing, in themselves they do, if they are carefully enough constructed, provide a useful orientation, or reorientation, of thought, such that an extended unpacking of them can be an effective way of developing and controlling a novel line of inquiry."[21]

Second, the attempt to define religion, to specify something that gives religion its identity as religion, need not focus on function. Indeed, prior to the appearance of nonconfessional approaches to the study of religion in the nineteenth and twentieth centuries, most definitions of religion were substantive definitions: they defined religion in terms of particular beliefs or practices (such as the familiar dictionary definition of religion as devotion to a supernatural power that created and controls the universe). There are definite dangers in this approach. One of the reasons that Luckmann champions a functional definition of religion, for example, is because it "avoids both the customary ideological bias and the 'ethnocentric' narrowness of the substantive definition of the phenomenon."[22]

But functional definitions have their weaknesses too. For one thing, they tend to be so broad that they threaten to lose contact with our use of the word "religion" in ordinary parlance. Thus, as a hypothetical example, if we are told that while all belief in the supernatural and the transcendent will disappear in the future, religion will still be as strong as ever in that something else will fulfill the same function, might we not be justified in complaining that it would be truer to ordinary usage to say that God—and religion—has died?

While both functional and substantive definitions of religion have their weaknesses, I have chosen to specify the essence or identity of religion in substantive terms. Thus, rather than describing the transformation of religion in terms of a *continuity of function but a change of content*, it will be necessary to find *both the continuity and the change in religion's content*. Simply put, this seems to me a much stronger and, hence, more interesting thesis. It means that the word "religion" will be used in a way closer to its use in our ordinary speech. The narrowness that tends to undermine substantive approaches will be mitigated here by the fact that I am concentrating on contemporary religion in the United States. I shall not pretend to be dealing with "religion in general"—whatever that might mean.

One should be aware from the outset that any attempt to show how the essential core of religion is preserved through radical changes will appear to involve "stacking the deck." We have already seen how the definition of religion is determined by the interests of the investigator. Thus, one who wishes to advance the transformation thesis will inevitably define religion in such a way that the essence of religion is what remains intact in the midst of various changes. But this hardly implies that the argument is no more than a meaningless sleight-of-hand. On the contrary, the argument may be genuinely enlightening if certain criteria are met, some of which have already been mentioned. The definition employed should have a significant connection with the traditional use of the term; the definition should focus on characteristics that are, at least by some measures, interesting and important; and the definition should help us explore territory that has not been thoroughly investigated before.

Given that I am interested in the fate of religion in contemporary first-world culture—and in the United States in particular, where Judaism and Christianity continue to be the most influential players—it is probably not surprising that I shall focus on belief in God. After all, even new religious movements that wish to break free from Judaism and Christianity—most notably various radical feminist religious currents—tend to draw on theism, however much they wish to transfigure it. Whether as God, Goddess, or innumerable goddesses, deity is at the center of our pieties.[23]

The task at hand, then, is to specify exactly what is meant by "God," so that in subsequent chapters it will be possible to determine how the notion of God is being transformed, i.e., how the identity of this notion is preserved in the midst of radical changes, changes that are in fact necessary precisely to preserve its identity. One could pile up an enormous number of qualities that have been attributed to God by Jews and Christians over the ages: God created the world freely; God is eternal; God is omnipotent; God is a jealous God; God parted the Red Sea; God is a mighty warrior, he is King and Lord; God brought the Great Flood upon the world; God will punish sin unto the second and third generation; God is forgiving; God continually sustains the world; God promises a peaceable kingdom as the world's destiny. This list barely scratches the surface, yet it suffices to show that it is no easy task to decide how we ought to define God. Even this brief list confonts us with potential contradictions—God as warrior and God as author of the Peaceable Kingdom, for example—and it includes qualities that many contemporary Jews and Christians might find dubious—that God is a jealous God, or that he parted the Red Sea. And things become more complicated when we include claims about God that separate Christianity and Judaism from one another: the key to devotion to God is obedience to his Torah; God is a Trinity; salvation requires that God become incarnate and die.

Clearly, there is no unchanging notion of God to be found in Jewish and Christian history. In fact, there may be only a loose connection, a "family resemblance," among many of the different approaches to God in Jewish and Christian piety.[24] It appears that transformation has been an ongoing part of the history of this notion, as well as being a part of its future. And it follows that, as with the attempt to define religion, our definition of the word "God" will necessarily be an interpretive decision, not a simple report on what is objectively the case. Yet this decision need not be arbitrary: it ought to continue the family resemblance with previous usage, so that one can immediately recognize a connection with traditional talk about God in Western theology, and it should be an interesting and useful definition, one that helps us investigate the dynamic of transformation that it is our task to explore here.[25]

Let us say that by "God" we intend *the transcendent source of life and meaning that ultimately informs the believer's every thought and action*. This is a God whom, in the words of the Jewish confession known as the Shema, we should love with our whole heart, our whole soul, and our whole might. This definition provides some definite boundaries. For example, it rules out any merely immanent object of devotion; we mean by "God" something that clearly transcends us. It dictates that God be that to which the believer looks for meaning and guidance, and this meaning and guidance is all-encompassing. To say that God "ultimately" affects all that the believer thinks and does is not to suggest that the believer consciously reflects on God with respect to every possible activity that the believer might undertake, but that, at least ideally, belief in God provides the overarching framework of meaning into which every activity fits. It is a framework that forms the basic disposition out of which the believer's specific thoughts and actions flow. This defintion of God also entails some form of monotheism, insofar as it speaks of *the* source of life and meaning, rather than many sources.[26]

To say that the notion of God is being transformed in contemporary piety is to claim that there are radical changes occuring in how persons think of God, but that the core of the notion, as specified in the definition given above, remains intact. In one sense, a good deal of modern theology has been taken up with the transformation of God. Theologians since Schleiermacher, awakened by Kant's critical philosophy to the problems connected with traditional notions of God as a supreme being or supernatural entity, have been working to transform our understanding of God's ontological status, i.e., the sense in which it can be said that God "is."[27] Schleiermacher spoke of God as the "whence of our feeling of absolute dependence,"[28] and he understood that feeling not as a simple relation of consciousness to an object, but as a dialectic—the feeling of absolute dependence negates the feeling of absolute freedom—thus safely removing God from the realm of objects.[29] Theologians such as Paul Tillich and Karl Rahner continued this work of transformation, especially insofar as they imbibed Heidegger's concern to distinguish Being from beings and applied it to the quest to understand the being of God.[30] An even more radical reworking of God's being was accomplished by the Jewish thinker Hermann Cohen, who took up the tenets of Kant's philosophy more directly: Cohen thinks of God neither as one being among others nor as being-itself, but as an ultimate rational ideal.[31]

But these acts of transformation have tended to be driven more by philosophical concerns than by larger social and religious forces.[32] As a result, they cannot easily be understood to represent a transformation of religion, but only of the notion of God considered as a discrete intellectual issue.[33] By contrast, I am taking the idea of God as the core of a particular form of religiosity, which means that the transformation of that idea can be effected not just by relatively isolated philosophical and theological considerations but by the larger forces that mold religion as a social phenomenon. And it means that, when the idea of God is transformed, this transformation is tantamount to a transformation of religion. We are seeking a deity whose metamorphosis takes place not just in the minds of theologians, but also at the intersection of powerful social currents. A new form of the divine cannot come into being, however, until the old one has passed away.[34]

↭ II ↭

The Subtle Demise of Traditional Theism

---

*F*undamentalists often suppose that by exactly repeating the formulations of previous centuries, they are preserving the essence of what was believed in those centuries. They fail to recognize that, because historical change brings with it genuinely different ways of seeing the world and of speaking about it, words authored in one historical environment will not mean the same thing when they are repeated in a different historical situation. Faithfulness to a tradition is not achieved, then, by continually reproducing the same formulations over and over again without change. This approach lacks historical consciousness. Rather, a tradition's adherents must constantly reinterpret the tradition's teachings so that what they meant in the past can still be heard and understood in a new setting.

While historical consciousness in its fullest form may be an achievement of the nineteenth century, there is a sense in which Jewish and Christian religious thinkers have always possessed it. The earliest rabbis understood that the Torah must continually be interpreted and applied to new circumstances. And Christian apologists have always reformulated the Gospel in terms of intellectual frameworks attractive to their contemporaries and to those persons they were attempting to missionize. In some cases the reinterpretations and reformulations may have been so extensive as to warrant talk of a transformation of belief: the essence of the tradition was preserved only by radically rethinking it. (Such a transformation may well have occurred, to cite but one example, in the events that led from the diverse and inchoate christologies of the New Testament to the complicated formulations of the Councils of Nicea and Chalcedon.[1])

One powerful indicator of the transformation of religion in our own day is the demise of traditional theism. By traditional theism I mean not belief in God as such—in that case the demise of this theism would signal not the transformation of belief in God but its destruction—but a particular form of belief in God. Traditional theism is belief in God as a supreme being. This God is understood as a supernatural personal agent, a transcendent consciousness who acts independently of human perceptions and projects. Traditional theism cannot be rejected lightly, at least not if one is concerned to preserve the essence of belief in God, for traditional theism has informed the beliefs of vast numbers of Jews and Christians up to the present day.

Why is traditional theism now supposedly in its death throes? A familiar and simplistic answer to this question is that it is just not possible to believe in the God of traditional theism in the present age. This God is, to begin with, inconsistent with the modern scientific world view. We can no longer conceive of an omnipotent consciousness independent of the physical universe of which we are a part. Anything that we can truly know must ultimately be explicable in terms of the statistically regular processes that make up our world. But there is a fundamental difficulty with the belief that traditional theism is no longer possible in the contemporary scientific era: while theologians and others have been confidently mouthing this contention for years, many well-educated, intelligent persons have apparently gone on affirming the notion of God championed by traditional theism— God as supernatural personal agent—unaware of any contradiction between their belief in this God and the other views that they necessarily imbibe as members of contemporary Western culture. The scientific world view does not seem to get in the way of their religious convictions, and the strictures of modern philosophical theologians against conceptions of God as a supreme being are even more remote from their consciousness.

If traditional theism is coming undone, it is not because it is impossible to embrace its concept of God, but because that concept can no longer be used in the way that it has been in the past. The concept of God as supernatural personal agent is now employed in a way that devastates the essence of the notion of God as it has been understood in Western piety. Put in terms of the definition of God proposed in the previous chapter, to utter the formulations of traditional theism in the contemporary environment is to abandon significant parts of the notion of a transcendent source of life and meaning that ultimately informs one's every thought and action.

Briefly stated, this is the dilemma facing the God of traditional theism: to affirm the idea of a supernatural personal agent consistently today is necessarily to embrace a privatized deity. Belief in God is no longer used to explain events taking place outside the private sphere in the larger arenas of nature and history. As we shall see below, this does not mean that the believer makes a conscious choice to think of God as of merely private significance; it is not a matter of altering the traditional Western notion of deity and attributing particular properties to God that render him irrelevant to history and nature.[2] Rather, the concept of God is simply not applied there. While traditional theism appears to be alive and well because many persons still subscribe to its concept of God, that concept is being used in a way wholly contrary to the meaning of the tradition. The God of traditional theism is dead after all.

Already in the previous chapter we noted that privatization is one of the hallmarks of the secularization process, and that it means that religion loses its ability to inform all dimensions of human activity, including public ones. But privatization is not a one-dimensional phenomenon. It will be useful to distinguish between what might be termed *structural privatization* and *conceptual privatization*. Structural privatization is a process whereby religion is taken out of the loop of social power, so that it has little ability to affect decisions made in the political and economic spheres of a particular society. By contrast, conceptual privatization means that the very notion of God implies or is understood in such a way that God is only relevant to the private dimension of existence (belief in God informs one's moral judgments, for example, and one's sense of personal well-being, but not one's relation to all dimensions of the world). The difference between the two types of privatization can be clarified by an example: early Christianity suffered structural privatization in the Roman Empire prior to Constantine. As a persecuted minority religion, it had no political power and no ability to directly influence public policy. But early Christian belief was not characterized by conceptual privatization, because even though Christians were out of the loop of social power, they conceived of their God as actively controlling historical events and as ultimately in charge of the destiny of Rome and the rest of the world. Roman religion—the cults officially endorsed by the Roman state—on the other hand, were neither structurally nor conceptually privatized.[3]

Contemporary sociologists of religion, guided by Max Weber's discussion of the rationalization of modern Western society, tend to describe all religion in the modern West, not just persecuted minority movements, as structurally privatized. The dynamics of rationalization, especially as a function of modern capitalism, have carved out various autonomous segments in society, each with its own rational norms. Independent, purely economic norms now hold sway in the economic realm—not the overarching values prescribed by a religion—and the same thing occurs in other segments of the social order. Whereas religion tended to hold the segments of Medieval society together and to dictate their collective goals, each segment of modern society sets its own goals, and religion thus finds itself confined to its own isolated sphere.[4]

But recall that structural privatization need not lead to conceptual privatization, at least if the example of Christianity in the early Roman Empire can be trusted. Of course structural privatization can exert strong pressures on religious consciousness, especially in the modern and contemporary environments where religion as such, not just a particular religion or group of religions, is structurally privatized. If one sees that religion has no official social and political power, it may be more difficult to think of God as in charge of all dimensions of human history. The relationship of religious consciousness to society's structural dynamics will be even more threatened if Marxian analyses of the relation between the segments of society are held to be true. In that case, religion is not only unable to control the economic sphere of modern society, it is powerfully beholden to that sphere. In the end, however, there is no necessary connection between the two forms of privatization; while structural privatization may make it more difficult for the believer to avoid conceptual privatization, it surely does not make the conceptual form of privatization inevitable.

All religions in the contemporary Western world are subject to structural privatization. But traditional theism, in addition to being subject to this form of privatization, necessarily entails conceptual privatization as well. The idea of God simply loses its relevance outside the private sphere. Why?

It may be that there are several answers to this question, but I wish to focus on one particular issue: a peculiarly contemporary form of the problem of theodicy. The problem of theodicy has agonized theists from the beginning of Western religions: if there is a God who is both omnipotent and wholly benevolent, why is there so much suffering and evil in the world?[5] In the Jewish and Christian traditions, the problem is symbolized by the figure of Job in the Hebrew Bible. But however difficult the problem of theodicy has been for the believer, Job and his spiritual descendants have usually been able to cope with the problem, if not to solve it. What is different about theodicy in the contemporary world, then?

Any successful method for dealing with theodicy involves conceptual control. The believer's world view is threatened by destruction when confronted with serious instances of evil and suffering. The challenge is to bring the threat under control, to turn potential cognitive chaos into order, by pulling it into line with the believer's notion of God.[6] Such control can take various forms, including the position articulated in the book of Job: Job is never given an explanation of why he has suffered, but he is apparently satisfied with the idea that he simply cannot comprehend God's ways. For even that idea, however unsatisfying to one who seeks thorough conceptual mastery of the problem, at least suggests that there *is* an explanation for evil and suffering, even if we are incapable of grasping it. This is still to preserve one's belief in God and to ward off chaos.

What is different about theodicy in contemporary technological society is that the problem of evil and suffering escapes any attempts to cognitively control it. This is so for at least three reasons. First, and most important I think, is the effect of contemporary communication technologies, especially television news. Television news graphically confronts us with events from every corner of the world as they happen. And this means that we are continually bombarded by images of every conceivable form of human suffering. It is not unusual to see, in one sitting, earthquake victims in one country, the carnage of a war somewhere else, and starving children in a third region of the world. The instances of evil and suffering are not only many, they are diverse. And it is this which explodes any conceptual scheme which seeks to contain them.

This peculiarly contemporary dilemma becomes clearer if we contrast it with the challenge of theodicy in previous epochs. Consider a paradigmatic example for the Western religions: biblical scholars isolate a particular tradition within the Hebrew Bible that they refer to as the "Deuteronomic history." The Deuteronomic historian looks back over the most catastrophic events that the people of Israel have suffered, the most important being the destruction of the Northern Kingdom by the Assyrians in the eighth century B.C.E. and the exile of the Southern Kingdom by the Babylonians in the sixth century B.C.E. These events can be explained, from the Deuteronomist's perspective, by interpreting them as punishments from God for the people's disobedience to his dictates and their failure to heed his warnings.[7] What the Deuteronomist must do, first, is to establish the basic principle that God will intervene in history to punish his people when they disobey him. Then he must turn to the actual events of suffering at issue and demonstrate how they fit this pattern, i.e., how they can be legitimately interpreted in terms of Israel's disobedience to divine commands and warnings. If his philosophy of history succeeds, then the events that have befallen the people of Israel no longer stand as threats to belief in God and the meaningfulness of human life. Control has been exercised over experiences that might have plunged the community into cognitive chaos.

This classic Jewish and Christian mechanism of theodicy, wherein particular events are interpreted as conforming to a pattern dictated by some principle of divine justice or providence, is made even clearer by contrasting it with the response to evil and suffering in a non-theistic religious world view. Consider the Azande response to misfortune, for example, as described in an esteemed study by E. E. Evans-Pritchard.[8] The Azande can apparently interpret almost any instance of things going awry as ultimately the result of witchcraft.[9] In Evans-Pritchard's words, "if . . . any failure or misfortune falls upon any one at any time and in relation to any of the manifold activities of his life it may be due to witchcraft."[10] If a woman injures her foot, if a man becomes ill, if one's hut burns down, if people are hurt when a granary collapeses upon them, witchcraft is almost inevitably suspected as an element in the chain of events. Thus, Evans-Pritchard can speak of "the variability, we may almost say the inconsistency, of witchcraft as a cooperating cause in the production of phenomena."[11] This lack of any discernable pattern should not be surprising. Witchcraft is not a unity; it may be practiced by many different persons with many different goals. It is by its very nature arbitrary and capricious, a result of sundry rivalries and hatreds. Traditional theism demands something quite different. If evil and suffering are to be grasped by reference to a single being who is both omnipotent and just, one must find some principle that can explain how evil and suffering might serve some larger, benevolent divine purpose. And one has to be able to believe that individual instances of suffering and evil fit the pattern dictated by this principle.[12]

The peculiarly contemporary form of the problem of theodicy consists in the fact that, while the believer can always posit some basic principle that explains how suffering and evil have a justifiable role in the divine scheme of things, the particular events with which the believer must deal can never all be fit securely under that principle.

For now the events are not confined to a particular place, people, time, or category. Contemporary information and communication technologies mean that we are confronted with an unceasing torrent of news about human suffering and evil of every possible kind. *It is not possible even to catalogue all of the instances of evil and suffering, let alone to correlate each of them with some human behavior that merits divine reproof or requires divine testing.* But if there is no hope of finding such a pattern in these events, then there is no sense in which they are meaningful and instructive. It will hardly help to say with Job that, while I cannot discern a pattern, I trust that the pattern exists in the mind of God. For however great Job's suffering, that suffering had definite boundaries. In fact, at least in the version of the story contained in the Hebrew Bible, Job's suffering is bounded by good fortune: his life begins with blessings and happiness, and it ends that way. The suffering is contained, and thus can be cognitively controlled. No such control is possible for the contemporary believer in front of the television set watching the evening news, for he or she is faced with endless evil and suffering.

A second dimension of the contemporary form of the problem of theodicy can be traced not to information technology, but to other types of technology. It is much harder to justify God in the face of human suffering when human beings themselves can now do so much to alleviate that suffering. Medical technology provides the clearest example. Polio was a horrifying disease that crippled countless children and adults. Before the advent of the polio vaccine, perhaps one could have thought of polio as somehow inevitable given the laws governing the natural world, or even as somehow part of an ultimately benevolent divine scheme. But once human beings found a way to prevent polio, the traditional theist's God was faced with a twofold problem: First, if men and women can now eliminate polio, why couldn't God have done so long ago, given that there is nothing inevitable or intractable about this disease? Second, it now seems evident that polio is not part of some mysterious divine plan, for polio has been, at least for the most part, taken out of the picture. Perhaps some hard-hearted theist will be tempted to say that both polio and its human elimination *were* part of a meaningful divine plan: God challenged human beings to grow by confronting them with the challenge of polio, including the challenge of finding a way to defeat it. But this is hardhearted indeed, for inumerable lives were devastated along the way, and those who triumphed in the struggle against the disease, such as Jonas Salk and the other members of the scientific community who perfected the polio vaccine, were usually not the ones who did the suffering. While such a God is not unthinkable, he is more a Darwinian deity seeking to coax a superman out of the mass of weak humanity than he is the New Testament God concerned with the fate of each sparrow; one would be hard pressed to regard him as the God of traditional Jewish or Christian theism.

The example of the polio vaccine is paralleled by numerous other cases. There are of course many examples within the arena of medical technology, but think also about how agricultural technologies can prevent starvation, about how the development of modern sanitation practices such as sanitary sewer systems for cities and towns and the regular removal of garbage from living areas has contributed to human health and increased life expectancy, and about how weather satellites and other meteorological tools can warn us about impending storms and save many lives. If we can take care of some of these things, why can't God? Or, if he *can* take care of them, why does he choose not to do so?

The third element to consider in the peculiarly contemporary form of the problem of theodicy is the twentieth century's proclivity for inflicting mass death.[13] The Armenian genocide, the Nazi Holocaust, the advent of nuclear weapons, the horrors instigated by Stalin and Pol Pot, all of these things confront contemporary persons with an incredibly dark picture of the human condition and humanity's potential fate. In some ways, this third element, for all of its mind-numbing horror, may not actually be as significant for theodicy as the first two elements. For one thing, these brutal acts are all instances of "man's inhumanity to man" rather than "acts of God," though it is hard to imagine a benevolent and powerful deity allowing them to happen. Furthermore, these acts are in some sense isolated. At least the human psyche often finds it possible to steer around them, to regard them as inexplicable black holes in the larger space of human events. But when they are added to the two elements discussed above, viz., the effect of being bombarded with stories of suffering and evil too numerous and diverse to fit into any pattern and the fact that human beings eliminate forms of suffering and evil that God does not, these events must surely take their toll on traditional theism.[14]

We must remember the point made earlier, however: there is nothing about the contemporary world that makes belief in God as supernatural personal agent impossible. On the contrary, many intelligent and compassionate persons seem to have no real difficulties in affirming this God's existence. The crucial point is not that the contemporary form of the problem of theodicy makes belief in traditional theism's God impossible, but that it radically alters the use, and thus the meaning, of that belief: its God may still be present in the convictions of inumerable believers, but traditional theism itself has disappeared. The traditional theist thought of God as a transcendent personal agent who acted within human history and oversaw the natural world that he had created. This God was identified with the idea of the transcendent source of life and meaning that ultimately informs the believer's every thought and action, the essential core of the Western notion of God. Of course the conception of God as personal agent has always raised the issue of theodicy. As the personal consciousness who exercises providence over nature and history, God must in some sense be responsible for what happens within those spheres. But, in the past, the theist could always find some pattern in events of suffering and evil that made it possible to see the events as part of a justifiable divine plan. The Deuteronomic history provides the paradigmatic instance of this for both Jews and Christians. Or, if one could not actually discern the pattern and articulate a theodicy, one could at least trust that some pattern did nonetheless exist. But the peculiarly contemporary form of the problem of theodicy places the God of traditional theism in a wholly new context, a context where the instances of suffering and evil are innumerable, patternless, and sometimes apparently more effectively addressed by human beings than by God.

This new context reorients the implications of traditional theism, and it does so in one of two ways. On the one hand, it can imply that God is evil. In other words, when even the hope of constructing a theodicy becomes impossible, then the personal agent responsible for both natural and human history can only be regarded as in some sense hostile. God is left without justification for his actions. But this route is simply impossible for the theist. Not only does it destroy the essential core of the notion of God, inasmuch as a hostile or even an indifferent God would not be the source of life and meaning to which a believer can look, but it suggests a kind of religious psychosis. One can live with either agnosticism or atheism, but what would it be like to truly believe that, in Shakespeare's words, "As flies to wanton boys are we to the gods; they kill us for their sport"?[15] The idea that all of life is controlled by a malevolent supernatural power is psychologically unproductive at best.

Thus, traditional theism finds itself forced onto another path: one can continue to affirm that God is a benevolent supernatural agent if one abandons the claim that God is directly involved in the larger events of nature and history, since it is with those events that one encounters the contemporary problem of theodicy. That is, it is not the instances of suffering that befall me as an individual that explode the possibility of theodicy. For those personal instances can all be fit into some coherent pattern; they are bounded and unified by the contours of my biography. The barrage of patternless instances of suffering to which information technologies subject me occurs not within the manageable confines of my own individual experience, but on the plane of world history and natural events. And the apparent absence of God brought into relief by human technological advances in fields such as medicine is, again, an absence from the natural world as it impinges upon human beings. Belief in God as personal agent, the God of traditional theism, is by no means impossible, but the contemporary context necessarily reworks that belief. This personal agent can only be benevolent and a source of meaning if its personal agency is essentially confined to the private sphere.

The theist can now think of God as sustaining his or her sense of the self and its significance, as a guide to moral behavior, and as the source of life after death for the individual soul. But this brand of belief is not a key for understanding the wider arenas of history and the natural world.[16] It should be noted, where moral guidance is concerned, that the theist's God can in fact inform moral behavior not just in the personal realm, but in the social arena as well. If the theist thinks of God as a loving father who cares for each individual soul, for instance, this may well lead the theist to embrace social policies that seem consistent with the God-given worth and dignity of each human being. The crucial point here, however, is that this is still a matter of human initiative: it is quite different from holding that *God* is acting in particular events and guiding history in a specifiable fashion. Indeed, the theist's approach to these issues of social morality and policy would inevitably be quite different if he or she believed that God himself were going to act decisively. In fact, one might well argue that an activist social ethic makes most sense where there is a relatively weak doctrine of divine providence.

The prophetic tradition in the Hebrew Bible may seem to contradict such an argument. Do not the prophets combine a powerful social ethic with an equally powerful doctrine of divine providence? Clearly in one sense they do, but note that this providence seems to operate at the boundaries of the nation's history more than through individual events within it. That is, the divine action about which the prophets warn is the destruction of the nation. This is even clearer in apocalyptic thinking: God acts decisively, but only to end history as a whole. Indeed, apocalyptic arises precisely at those points where one has given up on the possibility of history being redeemed from within, by either God or human beings. Apocalyptic is conceptual privatization's violent offspring.

In summary, then, we end up with this formula: the God of traditional theism, plus the contemporary context, equals conceptual privatization of God. Of course, as we noted earlier, the believer need not be conscious of this process. She or he certainly need not reconceptualize God by giving him particular properties that confine him to the private sphere, nor even reflect on the fact that God is no longer active outside that sphere. Rather, given the contemporary form of the problem of theodicy, traditional theism's God will simply no longer mesh with affairs beyond the private sphere; he can do no real work there. Thus, if we have already distinguished between structural privatization and conceptual privatization, we ought now to subdivide conceptual privatization into what can be termed *subjective* and *objective* conceptual privatization. Subjective conceptual privatization is a matter of the believer consciously viewing God as irrelevant for explaining events in the worlds of nature and history. By contrast, objective conceptual privatization is not itself a function of the believer's own consciousness, though it may bring subjective privatization in its wake. How can conceptual privatization, which is a matter of meaning rather than of social and material forces, be objective?

The answer to this question begins with the observation that meaning is not simply the result of subjective intent, a fact constantly reiterated by twentieth-century hermeneutics.[17] Meaning only occurs within a context. Words take on meaning through their relation to other words and in the context of grammatical rules for their use. Indeed, the contextual character of meaning extends all the way to the level of world views. The components of a world view are determined in their meaning by their relation to other elements of the world view. To take a very simple example, the assertion that one smokes three packages of cigarettes a day has a different meaning today than it had in 1940. The statement has specific health implications it would not have had in 1940 and, given the rancorous contemporary debates about the rights of nonsmokers to be protected from cigarette smoke as well as the estimates put forth as to the costs of smoking to the nation's health care system, the statement may even suggest something about the smoker's relation to the larger society which would not have been a part of its meaning in an earlier time.

In that the contemporary first-world environment brings with it a particularly potent, and finally insurmountable, version of the problem of theodicy, assertions about a benevolent supernatural agent can only make sense or have consistent meaning if the assertions are isolated from the historical and natural realms in which this problem of theodicy lies. In other words, the context of meaning leads to the conceptual privatization of traditional theistic notions. Whether the individual believer's own theology is sufficiently consistent that he or she is forced to reflect on this conceptual privatization is another matter; the kind of privatization at issue is, at least initially, objective rather than subjective.[18]

If the contemporary first-world environment does result in the conceptual privatization of traditional theism, the implications are far-reaching, for the conceptual privatization of the divine devastates the essential core of the notion of God. God is supposed to be the transcendent source of life and meaning that informs the believer's every thought and action. While the privatized God can inform one's *actions*, including one's actions as an individual in the public sphere, he cannot inform one's *thinking* in the way that the concept of God traditionally could: one does not look to the privatized God to explain what happens in the worlds of history and nature. And from this it follows that God is no longer the source of meaning that he once was. Even God's role as source of life is now significantly diminished inasmuch as the world of nature is a realm largely indendent of God.

But perhaps most surprising is the fact that the conceptually privatized God turns out, upon careful scrutiny, to fail the test of genuine transcendence. Transcendence suggests otherness, but not just any sort of otherness will do. It is not sufficient, for example, for God to be other simply in the sense of belonging in a category all his own. Divine transcendence, as it has been understood in the history of Western religion, entails not merely uniqueness over against all the categories of finite being, nor even just that God is not subject to any of the constraints that constitute finitude. That would be a merely negative kind of transcendence: God is what finite being is not. Rather, divine transcendence means that God surpasses every category of finite being precisely insofar as God creates, sustains, and guides every category of finite being; everything finite depends on God for both its essence and its existence. Thus, God must be immanent within every dimension of the finite, and actively so, in order to be truly transcendent.[19] To the extent that the conceptually privatized God is no longer actively involved within all the spheres of finite being, he is no longer transcendent. Stated more baldly, he is no longer God.

It turns out, then, that *the formulations of traditional theism, when repeated in the context of contemporary first-world culture, manifest real change amidst illusory continuity*: the concept of God is the same, but its different use gives it a wholly new meaning. The venerable concept of God as a supernatural personal agent, the Supreme Being, now destroys the essential core of the theology that it once expressed. This change in religion is not transformation, but dissolution. If God-centered religion is to be transformed, its essential core passed on in the midst of radical changes, I would contend that one requisite change will be the abandonment of the idea of God as personal agent. For it is the idea of God as personal agent, when it comes up against the peculiarly contemporary form of the problem of theodicy, that results in the destruction of the notion of God.

Reflection on this potentially surprising claim returns us to an observation made in the previous chapter: that arguing the transformation thesis will appear to involve something like "stacking the deck" when it comes to defining religion. Why couldn't one who wishes to hold on to belief in God as supernatural personal agent simply declare that to be part of the essence of the notion of God? In that case, one should maintain belief in God as personal agent, even though it now entails conceptual privatization, and abandon the idea of God as the transcendent source of life and meaning that informs the believer's every thought and action, rather than vice-versa. However, this very scenario reinforces the contention that the definition of God with which we have been operating is not in fact arbitrary or merely calculated to make the transformation thesis work in a certain way. Let us think for a moment about ordinary usage of the word "God." While the vast majority of Jews and Christians through the ages have thought of God as a personal agent, one can imagine God without that quality. In fact, though in the minority, there have always been voices in the Jewish and Christian traditions that have suggested that God is not really a personal being. Most notable among them are those philosophically inclined theologians who have seen personhood as all-too-human, and those mystics who have been more comfortable thinking of God as an all-encompassing absolute than as a supernatural person. But surely one would break with ordinary use of the term "God" altogether if one were to employ the word to refer to something that is not transcendent, and not the source of life and meaning that affects the believer's grasp of every dimension of the world. A being without these qualities, however powerful and extraordinary it might be, would more accurately be described, in good science fiction parlance, as a "superior life form" rather than as God.

The trajectory that religious transformation must take, given the contemporary situation, is clear: the idea of God as personal agent must be abandoned in order to preserve the essential core of the notion of God. But even if this abandonment is, in the end, unavoidable, we should approach it carefully. As already noted, while there have always been those who have conceived of God as other than personal, most Jews and Christians have taken the personal character of God to be a crucial attribute. That is why the change under investigation constitutes a thorough transformation of Western thinking about the sacred, and not simply a minor adjustment. In order to gauge the seriousness of this change, and to avoid the facile rejection of divine personhood familiar in some quarters, we ought to contemplate the strengths of the idea of God as a supernatural personal being.

First, if God is to be the fundamental source of meaning for the believer's life, it is particularly appropriate to think of God as personal. Some of the deepest dimensions of the human self are engaged only in interpersonal relationships. For example, while we can speak of "loving" all sorts of things, it is really only other persons who can be the focus of our love in the fullest sense of the term. And if part of what is entailed in finding a sense of meaning is believing that one's life matters, that it has some point beyond the confines of one's own ego, then it is important that there be some other to deem one valuable. The notion of God as an impersonal Absolute will hardly do here, for only another consciousness can genuinely value us; to say that we are valued by an abstract One would be entirely and self-deceptively metaphoric. It is not surprising, then, that even in religions that put a geat deal of emphasis on the divine as essentially an unknowable Absolute, powerful movements toward a more personal conception of deity inevitably break out (as in the bhakti traditions within Indian religion).[20]

Second, prayer is in danger of losing all meaning if God is not taken to be personal. For prayer in the Western tradition is clearly meant to be interpersonal communication. One could always pray to an impersonal deity as a kind of meditational device, but only if God is a consciousness can prayer mean what it has traditionally meant in Judaism and Christianity. And if one cannot genuinely pray to his or her deity, then it is difficult to understand how this deity can be the "very present help in trouble" that devout Jews and Christians have usually taken God to be.[21]

As a third consideration, we come to something that is arguably at the very heart of all religion. It is evident that the consciousness of death has a singular importance in how human beings decide to live their lives.[22] Even in the ancient world, long before modern European constructions of the individual self, the hero of the Gilgamesh epic agonized over his own inevitable death, not just over the fate of the larger group of which he was a part.[23] At the other end of the historical spectrum, where one might expect that the postmodern dissolution of the subject had robbed the consciousness of death of its power, we find postmodernism's most influential thinker, Jacques Derrida, confessing that "All my writing is on death. . . . If I don't reach the place where I can be reconciled with death, then I will have failed. If I have one goal, it is to accept death and dying."[24] Certainly religion has always been centrally concerned with death. Harold Bloom goes so far as to proclaim that "religion, whether it be shamanism or Protestantism, rises from our apprehension of death."[25]

The most straightforward way in which the Western religions have dealt with the anxiety of death is by believing that the individual self survives death and enjoys eternal life with God. It is an unexpected truth that the contemporary scientific world view, far from creating difficulties for traditional theism on this matter, dictates that the notion of the continued existence of the human subject after death is only possible in the context of belief in God as a personal supreme being. In the past, one might have supposed that the human self was naturally immortal, and that the self would thus survive death without any supernatural intervention. But contemporary science and our own daily experience in the contemporary world work together to convince us that, whatever the self is, it is absolutely dependent on the physical body. That which defines our subjectivity, our very personality, is not some immortal soul that can float free from the physical moorings of the brain. On the contrary, the personality can be directly affected and even permanently altered by changes in the chemistry and structure of the brain: surgery on the brain, trauma to it, the ingestion of certain kinds of drugs, Alzheimer's disease, and countless other purely physical phenomena can radically change who we are. If death is the end of brain and body, and if our personality and subjectivity are thoroughly dependent upon, if not simply identical with, this brain and body, then there is no chance that the human subject can survive death.

Unless, of course, we are graced by some supernatural intervention that re-creates us after death. This is precisely what is promised in the original Jewish and Christian notions of resurrection. While Christianity later took up the idea of the immortality of the soul, it is the earlier conception of life after death as resurrection, as miraculous re-creation by God, that is required here. And such miraculous re-creation presupposes that there exists a personal supreme being, for only a personal consciousness can graciously decide to purposively intervene in the natural causal order, and only a supreme being has the power to re-create a human person beyond the bounds of time and space. Thus, while other forms of belief in God may be able to offer some comfort in the face of death, only traditional theism has a God who can provide the literal survival of the individual subject after the demise of the body.

Suppose one were to reply that, while it is indeed the case that only traditional theism can provide genuine life after death, the focus on life after death is something religion is better off without. Perhaps death has always preyed on the psyche, but it is nonetheless true, so some have argued, that too much concern with death and afterlife distracts us from our duties in the here and now. And there certainly is more than a hint of selfishness in agonizing over the fact that one's own individual ego will cease to exist at some indeterminate point in the future, even though the rest of the world will remain intact. For this reason it is important to recognize that traditional theism stands alone not only in its ability to assure the individual life after death, but also in its power to guarantee a happy destiny for the whole human race. There is obviously nothing about the natural order that dictates that the human project will turn out well. On the contrary, it is entirely possible that human history will end in some gigantic Auschwitz, or be snuffed out in a planet-wide natural disaster. But once again the traditional theist's God adds a crucial extra dimension to the picture. This God exercises providence over history and sees to it that, however many horrific detours human history may take, it will eventually end up in the Kingdom of God. Our collective destiny is not Auschwitz, but the New Jerusalem. Just as in the case of life after death, this is only possible if there exists a supreme being, a personal consciousness who can miraculously intervene in the finite order.

All of these considerations should make it clear that the demise of God as supernatural personal agent is, in many ways, a grievous loss. The suggestion that his death should be greeted with Dionysian reveling is as often a manifestation of bad faith and false bravado as it is of a genuine affirmation of human life. But for good or for ill, the contemporary context spells the end of traditional theism and its picture of God as supernatural personal agent.

∽ III ∽

Continuity in Change:
God Transformed

*T*he transformation of the sacred—which in Western piety is equivalent to the transformation of God—entails not just the negative moment of abandoning the idea of God as personal supernatural agent, but also the positive moment of reclaiming the whole of human experience and activity as the domain of divine influence. Rejecting God as personal agent, then, is a necessary but not a sufficient condition for transformation; it does not automatically imply that conceptual privatization of some other type has been avoided. If we consider the progressive philosophical theologies initiated by Schleiermacher, we discover that they tend to abandon the notion of God as supernatural personal agent (though they do not leave behind all symbolic ties to the idea of a personal God).[1] How do these theologies fare, then, with regard to the problem of conceptual privatization?

One might initially be suspicious of their ability to ward off conceptual privatization, inasmuch as many of them—especially those most indebted to the unalloyed spirit of modernity—tend to take their point of departure not from an attempt to discern the objective structures of the world, but from the exigencies of human subjectivity. Following the famous "turn to the subject" by which Descartes initiated modern Western philosophy and its obsession with epistemology, Schleiermacher and his progeny have looked to the human subject as the key to talking about God.[2] This need not imprison God-talk in the private sphere however; it only dictates that one must always view reality from the vantage point afforded by the structures of human being. It is quite possible to survey many, if not all, dimensions of reality from that perspective. To take but one example, Paul Tillich, under the influence of the early Heidegger and other modern philosophers, undertakes a phenomenological ontology. That is, his starting point is the way in which things are given in human experience, but he regards this as a way to get at not just human being but the whole of reality. Indeed, it is his avenue to being-itself and, thus, to God.[3] And, as a matter of fact, far from relating God only to the personal sphere, Tillich has a great deal to say about God's relation to the world of nature. The last part of his *Systematic Theology* provides, among other things, an intricate, if not always convincing, theology of nature.[4]

Potentially more problematic for theologies like those of Schleiermacher and Tillich is something that may seem to imply that conceptual privatization is simply unavoidable: precisely insofar as God is conceived in these theologies *not* as a supernatural personal agent, but in much more absract terms, God cannot be expected to intervene in human history at particular points in time and space. But then what is God's relevance to the social and political spheres? If God is conceived in good Tillichian fashion as equally the ground of all events, or in a more decidedly postmodernist mode as the "divine milieu in which all things arise and pass away," no more or less present in one historical event than in another, then it is not clear that belief in God will have much power to inform one's judgments and activities within the social and political domain.[5] Are we in a no-win situation, then, a theological

Catch-22? Is it the case that belief in God as personal agent leads to conceptual privatization in the contemporary context, but that God conceived as impersonal also dictates at least some measure of privatization, insofar as an impersonal God cannot be linked to particular events in the social and political spheres?

Perhaps things are not quite so bleak. For Tillich's work demonstrates that God conceived as ground of being, rather than as a supernatural personal agent who can intervene in human history, can at least have a negative relevance to social and political affairs. The manner in which Tillich's God transcends all human events, serving not only as their infinite ground but also as their "abyss," allows the believer to judge idolatrous tendencies in history.[6] To take an example that is relevant to Tillich's own experience in Hitler's Germany, Tillich's theological perspective can show how attachment to one's nation, when it becomes a matter of ultimate concern, is tantamount to idolatry and will inevitably have destructive consequences. A cursory examination of the kind of philosophical theology initiated by Schleiermacher suggests, then, that such a theology can be developed in ways that combat conceptual privatization. Yet it is not automatically and unambiguously protected from conceptual privatization simply because it rejects the conception of God as personal agent.

Another theological current that deserves mention is process theology. At its best, as in the work of John Cobb, process theology is an impressive intellectual achievement. Cobb and others have brilliantly adapted the philosophy of Alfred North Whitehead to the needs of Christian theology.[7] Process theology may appear to show a way around the dilemma we are exploring; it seems to be able to hold onto the conception of God as personal agent without incurring the penalties that the contemporary form of the problem of theodicy exacts upon traditional theism. The unusual move that the process theologians make is to drop the notion of divine omnipotence. Their limited God, the "fellow-sufferer who understands," in Whitehead's famous phrase, is not responsible for the innumerable instances of suffering and evil that undermine the natural and historical worlds, for he is simply unable to prevent them.[8] At the same time, this God is a personal agent who attempts to influence events in all dimensions of reality. He cannot coerce human beings or other constituent elements of reality to do the good, but he constantly lures them to the good, urging them on by appealing to their own freedom.[9]

The central problem here, where conceptual privatization is concerned, is that process theology's assertion of divine agency is ambiguous, if not simply empty. What is the cash value of the claim that, while God cannot control events, he lures them on? Where do we actually see this divine activity, and how would things look different if it were not present? In other words, the idea that God always acts through creaturely freedom, and never miraculously breaks into history or nature, rending the fabric of ordinary causality, seems an unfalsifiable assertion. By firmly ensconcing God's alleged activity within the freedom of his creation, process theology has hidden God's action so effectively that the very notion of divine activity becomes ambiguous, or perhaps even vacuous. This central problem is compounded by the familiar complaint that if one limits God as severely as process theology does, one is left with no God at all, but only a "puny godling," in John Macquarrie's telling phrase.[10] This diminutive deity may vitiate that essential core of divine attributes that we are attempting to preserve. Furthermore, the price of admission into the inner sanctum of process theology is acceptance of an elaborate Whiteheadian metaphysic. If this particular metaphysic is unconvincing, then it is not possible even to begin to consider what process theology has to say about God's activity.

One other theological current that ought to be mentioned is Latin American liberation theology, as represented in the work of Gustavo Gutierrez, for example.[11] Surely one would not expect to find conceptual privatization here, for liberation theology's defining concern is to apply the Christian gospel to social and political liberation.[12] But this liberation theology is, according to its own understanding, a peculiarly third-world effort. It is supposed to arise out of the experience and struggle of the oppressed in Latin America. As a result, it cannot effectively be applied to the first-world dilemma that we are exploring.

Evidence of this is found in the fact that liberation theologians appear to be simply uninterested in the task of spelling out in a critical fashion what they mean by God's liberating activity within history. The Exodus is typically taken in liberation thought as the paradigmatic instance of this activity. But there is no suggestion that liberation theologians expect God to match the parting of the Red Sea by literally destroying the guns of today's oppressors, or that they think that he will miraculously put manna in the mouths of the poor. It may be simply unnecessary for the Latin American theologians to consider these things, given what this theology is meant to accomplish in its own environment. But in the context of the concerns with which we are dealing, liberation theology's notion of divine activity becomes disturbingly ambiguous. One can imagine a secular political activist saying to the liberation theologian, "I share every one of your political goals, but I don't understand what God-talk adds to your efforts, other than a purely psychological boost. Explain to me exactly what you expect God to do that is distinguishable from our own actions to combat oppression." The Vatican makes essentially the same point, though obviously from an entirely different perspective.[13] In addition, while liberation theologians affirm God's relevance to the social and political segments of human affairs, they clearly still conceive of God as a personal agent, and they do so without convincingly addressing the peculiarly contemporary form of the problem of theodicy (which problem is, of course, more relevant to the first-world situation).[14]

Given the ambiguity of where these various theologies stand vis-à-vis conceptual privatization, it behooves us to look for a theological approach that more straightforwardly attacks privatization. Such an approach can be found, I think, in a particular current of contemporary feminist religious thought. In addition to its unambiguous escape from conceptual privatization, this current of thought has the advantage of offering a radical approach to the being of God. This is useful, not because there is any value in radicality for its own sake, but because it helps to more clearly delineate the paradox of transformation: some elements of the concept of God may undergo vast and surprising changes, but these very changes may allow us to hold on to what is essential in our thinking about God.

It seems to me that there is an implicit motif in much feminist theology according to which God is a relation that human beings choose to enact. This does not entail reducing the divine in Feuer-bachian fashion to an unconscious, alienating projection or dismissing it as a mere imaginary entity. On the contrary, essential constituent elements of the divine may genuinely transcend the human—both "nature" and the "power of being" are familiar candidates in feminist thought—and one actualizes a relation to them consciously and in a way that is productive not of alienation but of *metanoia*, a positive transformation of the self.[15] But neither is God conceived in this cur-rent of feminist theology as an independent reality. Human beings do not simply enact a relation to the divine; they enact the divine itself, insofar as Goddess *is* a particular transformative relationship between the self and nature, the power of being, and other selves.

At the same time, there is no hint here of the autonomous, overconfident self of the modernists. It is not a matter of a monadic subject, having fully formed itself *ex nihilo*, subsequently deciding to enact divinity. Rather, the pattern seems much closer to Martin Buber's observation that the "I" is formed by the relations in which it is engaged: the "I" of the "I-It" relation is a different "I" from the "I" of the "I-Thou" relation.[16] Human beings choose to enact the divine, but they are to a large degree creatures of this relation and not just its creators.

To say that human beings choose to "enact" the divine seems to convey the proper sense, then. The word "enact" can mean, first of all, to legislate, which carries a creative, active sense, and that is part of what I want to highlight about the feminist reformulation of the divine. But "enact" can also mean to put on a play, in which case the persons who "act" are not acting as autonomous egos but are the vehicles for something else: the identities that they are representing on stage. Similarly, to enact the divine is to actualize the self's cre-ative powers at the same time that the self is formed by something beyond itself.

Buber's interpretation of the I-Thou relationship can be used not only as a key to how the self is formed as it enacts the divine, but also as a model or analogue for the phenomenon of enactment itself: just as the relation enacted between I and Thou is not something unreal and merely external to I and Thou, so the relation to be discussed here, a relation enacted between the self and nature, other selves, and the power of being, is something very real and something more than the sum of its constituent elements. Indeed, this relation *is* the divine (in contrast to the more traditional perspective that results from Buber's own theological extrapolations from his I-Thou anthropology, according to which God is not a relation that human beings enact, but one of the poles in a relation, the Eternal Thou).

Feminist theology is obviously not a monolithic movement. There are many types of feminist religious thought, and tensions surely exist between different feminist theological camps, tensions indicated by labels such as "reformers" and "revolutionaries" or "feminists" and "womanists." Yet the radical ontological motif of interest here seems to cut across some of these divisions: its traces can be found as easily in the thought of Rosemary Radford Ruether as in that of Carol Christ. Of course, following up these traces will entail more than simply summarizing the works of various feminist thinkers; my interpretation will of necessity be a constructive one, especially since feminist theologians have not been particularly concerned to unpack the ontological implications of their God-talk.[17] Furthermore, because I am interested in the continuities as well as the changes that characterize the transformation of the divine, my interpretations will sometimes find Goddess in places where she is not often sighted by the more radical feminist thinkers (the realms of history and ethics, for example). I shall lay the groundwork for this constructive reading by attempting to work out the logic behind the motif that I want to highlight. Then it will be possible to look at particular thinkers and themes in order to flesh out this abstract logic.

The logic at issue begins with the familiar observation that traditional male theologies are ideological. These theologies invariably employ male images to describe God—Father, Lord, King—and such images reflect and reinforce patriarchal power. One response to this observation might be to embrace an abstract philosophical perspective that promises to take us beyond ideological descriptions of the divine. From this perspective one supposedly recognizes that God is a transcendent reality that cannot be modeled in terms of human attributes and experiences. We cannot rely on human gender categories in our attempt to understand God. Instead, we must reach for abstract formulations such as the identification of God with being-itself. Or perhaps we should rest content with an apophatic theology, according to which we can only say what the divine is not, never what it is.

The suggestion here is that a carefully wrought philosophical theology can protect us from ideologically motivated notions of God. But a thorough-going feminist is bound to ask whether this isn't all a bit naive. Why should we assume that the philosophical vantage point from which we are trying to root out ideology is not itself ideological? This line of questioning uncovers an interesting paradox: a feminist might attempt to reveal masculine imagery for God to be ideological and inadequate by arguing that God's radical transcendence gives the lie to any description of the divine drawn from the realm of human experience. But this very notion of divine transcendence might be a peculiarly male creation, an expression of the assumption that the hierarchical structure of patriarchal society mirrors the divine-human relationship.

Thus, the attempt to avoid patriarchal ideology by eschewing all gender-specific imagery and insight in favor of philosophical abstractions soon breaks down. This is not to say that all descriptions of divinity are necessarily ideological, nor even less that all uses of reason are ideologically deformed, but only that this particular and familiar philosophical avenue turns out to be a dead end. But this is hardly the route that a committed feminist would choose in any case, for the feminist religious thinker typically wants to accomplish more than simply the negative task of removing destructive patriarchal elements from our notion of the divine. She wants, in addition, to find a notion of divinity that valorizes women's experiences and that empowers women in their spiritual, social, and political quests. Hence the decision to draw directly and unapologetically from women's experience in the attempt to talk about the divine. Most feminist theologies will make no effort, then, to be disinterested or naively objective: they will be self-consciously interested and perspectival, rooted in women's histories, experiences, and aspirations.

This methodological decision nonetheless requires justification. For on what grounds do we assume that this self-consciously interested perspective will provide an accurate reflection of divinity? Of course, this perspective is probably no more problematic than any other interested perspective. Indeed, it will not be open to the charge of ideology in the same way that traditional male theology is, for, in patriarchal societies, women's experiences are not a function of entrenched power. But this does not mean that the feminist perspective tells us about the reality of God. However sound the feminist theological agenda may be in terms of the quest for justice, we cannot blithely suppose that what ought to be the case about God is in fact the case. Is feminist theology condemned, then, to escape the Marxian critique of religion as ideology only to fall prey to the Freudian critique of religion as illusion?[18]

This challenge sets up the final step in the logic of feminist religious thought: it makes clear where the trajectory of feminist theology ultimately leads, ontologically speaking. The feminist perspective can be defended against the Freudian charge of illusion by arguing that the charge misunderstands feminist theology's notion of divinity. The Freudian critique rests on the assumption that the religious person believes in a God who is a supernatural reality independent of the self. Because this belief is a function of what the individual wishes to be the case rather than a matter of reason and evidence, it must be dismissed as an illusion. However, theology need not conceive of God as a reality independent of human sensibilities and projects, but can understand God instead as a reality that is actualized through those sensibilities and projects. Again, *the divine is a relation that human beings decide to enact.* Theology's task, then, is not to gain access to and make claims about some objective entity that it naively supposes is "out there," but to actualize the divine. This claim follows naturally upon the feminist inclination to pursue a theology that is, in the fullest sense of the phrase, a theology "from below," a theology that is openly a function of women's experiences and goals. In short, what women in their quest for justice wish to be the case is, quite appropriately, constitutive of the divine.

This conception of Goddess as a relation enacted by human beings goes well beyond the vision of the ultimate found in thinkers such as Heidegger and Tillich. Granted, both Heidegger and Tillich envision a nonobjective ultimate, and both tie the ultimate to the human subject. For the early Heidegger, one can only talk about *Sein* in relation to *Dasein*. And, for Tillich, one can only make sense of being-itself by reference to human being, through which being-itself is manifest as courage, the triumph over the threat of nonbeing. But both the relation between *Sein* and *Dasein* and that between being-itself and human being have an element of structural necessity about them that does not characterize the relationship between human beings and the sacred suggested by feminist theology. From the feminist perspective that we are exploring, human beings *choose* to enact the divine.

Hegel's panentheism, in which it is human thinking that brings the Absolute to full self-consciousness, is similarly not a true precedent of enactment theology, for Hegel's is a necessary process, not one human beings choose to initiate. While the Absolute requires human consciousness as a vehicle through which to realize itself, this process is nonetheless largely independent of human freedom, and the Absolute must therefore be regarded as self-originating, a *causa sui*. By contrast, to say that human beings can choose to enact the divine is to suggest that God is not self-originating, however much God may finally transcend the human beings who enact God.

Having explored the general logic leading to the enactment model of deity, we must turn to specific positions staked out by particular feminist thinkers, beginning with their commitment to a pragmatic theological method. To embrace a pragmatic method is to decide that one's criterion of truth will not be based on abstract considerations wholly internal to thought itself, but rather on a consideration of what perspective will be most effective in helping one to achieve certain practical goals. A radically pragmatic theological method, i.e., one that *begins* from pragmatic principles, implies one of two things: either the theologian has fallen prey to illusion in the Freudian sense, championing a self-originating deity who conveniently conforms to the theologian's wishes; or one recognizes that the divine is not self-originating but is something that human beings decide to enact.

But isn't there a third alternative, something between these two extremes? Suppose that we conceive of Goddess as self-originating, yet radically immanent. This deity would be intimately connected with our own being. Perhaps in this case we could argue that our own wishes for justice and our projects on its behalf do provide insight into the reality of the divine, but that our projects do not themselves enact the divine. This Goddess is sufficiently immanent for us to assume that our quest for justice mirrors her being, but ontologically independent at least to the degree that she is not beholden to human beings for her existence.

But how do we know that there *is* such a Goddess in the first place? If a theology is radically pragmatic, that is, if it uses pragmatic principles as its starting point, then it will have to make this decision too on pragmatic grounds. But then we must ask all over again on what grounds we can assume that our wishes and projects can tell us about the nature of Goddess (unless of course Goddess is acknowledged to be not just accessible through those wishes and projects but in some sense a function of them).

There is an all-important difference between a radical theological pragmatism and a pragmatism directed toward the natural world. In the latter case, the existence of the reality one seeks to know is not at issue. A pragmatist philosopher will probably point out that one never knows the world in and of itself apart from our projects, but the world is nonetheless a given, and it even asserts its independence by resisting some of our projects to shape it. No matter how useful or intellectually imaginative it might be to deny the phenomenon we call gravity, for example, I will still fall if I step off the top of the Empire State Building. There is no such givenness or resistance in the theological realm. As a result, we confront the notorious fact that there are almost no characteristics of divinity upon which all investigators are forced to agree: the divine will is invoked by pacifists and by advocates of nuclear war, and deity can easily be thought as one, many, or nonexistent.

It turns out, then, that the proposed third alternative, focused on an immanent deity that is nonetheless self-originating, cannot issue consistently from a theology that begins with pragmatic principles, but only from a theology that starts with a notion of God derived from authority, or tradition, or faith, or argument, or some other source, and only subsequently brings pragmatic principles to bear.

Some of the most influential feminist theologies have a pragmatic starting-point. This does not necessarily mean that the thinkers who have created these theologies subscribe to a particular school of philosophical pragmatism. Rather, it is a general methodological tendency that is at issue here: these thinkers self-consciously intend to construct images of the divine that will empower women, and this is their primary criterion—their starting point—for determining what they take to be the truth about deity. Of course, we can uncover some connections between various feminist theologies and particular schools of philosophical pragmatism. Some feminist theologians do after all make explicit use of pragmatist thinkers. Rebecca Chopp, for instance, draws on the work of Charles Peirce.[19] And John Dewey's famous pragmatist dictum that "the hypothesis that works is the true one" certainly applies to the feminist methodological bent that is of interest here.[20] Furthermore, both William James and John Dewey, when they speak about religion, think of their pragmatic criterion of truth as a matter not of abstract intellectual usefulness, but as one of existential or moral usefulness, and thus clear the ground for how feminist theologians employ a pragmatic method. James claims that religion produces consequences "useful to life,"[21] and Dewey links faith with the project of unifying the self and striving for our moral ideals.[22] But the specifics of James' pragmatism are tied up with his "radical empiricism," as the specifics of Dewey's pragmatism are tied up with his "empirical naturalism," and it is thus not to be expected that feminist theologians will necessarily want to embrace these specifics or those of any other school of philosophical pragmatism.

Rosemary Radford Ruether's *Sexism and God-Talk* provides a good example of this pragmatic methodological bent. Images of deity, she explains, "must be transformative."[23] This is consistent with what Ruether terms the "critical principle of feminist theology": "whatever diminishes or denies the full humanity of women must be presumed not to reflect the divine . . . ." Put positively, "what does promote the full humanity of women is of the Holy, it does reflect true relation to the divine, it is the true nature of things . . . ."[24]

Ruether is certainly not alone here. Mary Daly, in her classic manifesto of feminist theological consciousness, *Beyond God the*

Father, suggests a "pragmatic yardstick or verification process" for God-language: "In my thinking, the specific criterion which implies a mandate to reject certain forms of God-talk is expressed in the question: Does this language hinder human becoming by reinforcing sex-role socialization? Expressed positively. . . . Does it *encourage* human becoming toward psychological and social fulfillment, toward an androgynous mode of living, toward transcendence?"[25]

This same pattern—wherein one articulates both a negative and a positive form of a fundamental pragmatic principle—is found in Elisabeth Schüssler Fiorenza's approach to feminist Christian biblical interpretation. She holds that a feminist critical hermeneutics must "reject those elements within *all* biblical traditions and texts that perpetuate, in the name of God, violence, alienation, and patriarchal subordination, and eradicate women from historical-theological consciousness. At the same time, such a feminist critical hermeneutics must recover *all* those elements within biblical texts and traditions that articulate the liberating experiences and visions of the people of God."[26] The pragmatic starting-point is clear: "The revelatory canon for theological evaluation of biblical androcentric traditions and their subsequent interpretations cannot be derived from the Bible itself but can only be formulated in and through women's struggle for liberation from all patriarchal oppression."[27]

A similar pragmatic hermeneutical principle can be found in Judith Plaskow's critical reinterpretation of Judaism. The authority that grounds her critique is "the experience of particular communities struggling for religious transformation."[28] The particular community to which she is beholden is the Jewish feminist community and its quest for justice for women. To turn to its struggles as the source of authority and the criterion for one's theological project is, of course, to embrace a pragmatic theological method.

Carol Christ provides yet another example of a pragmatic approach. As Sallie McFague observes, "Christ's pragmatic position is illustrated by her lack of concern whether the Goddess is *entirely immanent* or also transcendent; what matters is the power for self-definition that it gives to women, its focus as a unifying symbol of female power."[29] It is worth noting how McFague's formulation hints at the connection between a thorough-going pragmatism and one's position on the ontological status of the divine: a strong pragmatism suggests that deity may not be "out there," independent of our projects.

If a pragmatic methodological bent is central to the whole notion of enacting the divine, so too is the concept of divine immanence. Not every theology that emphasizes divine immanence implies that we enact the divine, but any perspective which claims that we enact the divine will have to embrace divine immanence. We have already seen that immanence and transcendence are more tightly interwoven than often assumed;[30] so what is at issue is not enactment theology's immanence, but its transcendence. There will necessarily be an emphasis on immanence in such a theology, as there is in all theologies preserving the essential core of the Western notion of deity, but for different reasons. In the case of enactment theology, immanence occurs insofar as Goddess arises out of our own experiences, goals, and actions. But there can be a transcendent dimension as well in enactment theology, in at least two ways. First, as we shall see later on, the individual elements that human beings bring together in enacting the divine may transcend the human. Second, the relation that is enacted will itself surely surpass the individuals who effect it. Indeed, as was suggested above by reference to Buber's philosophy of the "I," the human self may end up, in some sense, being formed by the relations that it enacts. Thus, an enactment theology may be able to speak of Goddess transcending the finite by acting within it to empower and transform human beings.

Despite these very real elements of transcendence, some of the traditional supernatural attributes of divinity, which have typically (if erroneously) been identified with transcendence, will most likely disappear in any enactment theology. A Goddess who is beholden to us for her being and thus rooted in the finite, natural world cannot be conceived as a supernatural individual who can step in from beyond the finite world and violate its constitutive principles. For instance, we cannot expect, from the vantage point of this theology, to be resurrected from the dead.

A move away from traditional Western images of transcendence and toward a sense of the divine as immanent is a central impulse in contemporary feminist theology, as Judith Plaskow and Carol Christ make clear in their editorial remarks in *Weaving the Visions*.[31] Feminist theologians are critical of traditional male theologies that so often end up, in Rebecca Chopp's words, "reifying God."[32] Indeed, one of the most powerful reasons women have for focusing on the image of the Goddess rather than on a male image to symbolize the divine is of course that the Goddess suggests something more immanent to them, not because femaleness necessarily implies immanence, but simply because Goddess is of their own gender.[33]

In *Beyond God the Father*, Mary Daly provides a succinct formulation of the principle of immanence in feminist theology: "In hearing and naming *ourselves* out of the depths, women are naming *toward* God . . . ."[34] Later on, she develops this emphasis on immanence and speaks of "the Goddess within"[35] and points to "a sense of power, not of the 'wholly other,' but of the Self's be-ing."[36]

Another example of feminist theology's commitment to immanence is found in Carol Christ's description of women's religious experience:

"Awakening" is perhaps a more appropriate term than "conversion" for describing women's mystical experience, because "awakening" suggests the self needs only to notice what is already there. Awakening implies that the ability to see or to know is within the self, once the sleeping draft is refused. Conversion often seems to imply that one has turned from one source of authority to another, for example, from materialism to God. It seems to be characteristic of women's awakening that the great powers, while larger than the self, are within as well as without.[37]

All of this implies a rejection of the traditional image of the divine as a supernatural individual who can stand outside the finite. In the words of Naomi Goldenberg, feminists ought to "radically depart from . . . all systems of thought that posit transcendent, superhuman deities."[38] At the same time, there is a type of transcendence that can be combined with the emphasis on immanence so essential to feminist theology, a fact illustrated by Rosemary Radford Ruether's thought. Ruether rejects the transcendent, imperial God of patriarchal Christianity in favor of "the root human image of the divine as the Primal Matrix, the great womb within which all things, Gods and humans, sky and earth, human and nonhuman beings, are generated. . . . Here the divine is not 'up there' as abstracted ego, but beneath and around us as encompassing source of life and renewal of life."[39] In this image of what Ruether would have us name "God/ess," the divine is clearly immanent, but also all-encompassing, also transcendent to some degree.[40] The term "Primal Matrix" suggests an embracing framework or ground, something beyond us, of which we are nonetheless a part.

While none of these examples of the feminist commitment to divine immanence demands to be interpreted in terms of the enactment model of divinity, each of the examples is fully consistent with the enactment model. And we should not overlook the radical implications that these thinkers themselves sometimes draw from their commitment to divine immanence. Most notable in this regard is the suggestion, clearly articulated by both Ruether and Christ, that religious persons should abandon the notion of life after death.[41] One might well argue that the rejection of the traditional emphasis on life after death by feminist thinkers such as Ruether and Christ does imply something about the being of the divine. A divinity who does not deliver us from death perhaps *cannot* deliver us. And she cannot because she is rooted in nature and the finite. One can usefully think of a continuum of positions on life after death, and show how each position corresponds to a particular notion of the being of God: traditional Christian theism puts great emphasis on a literal restoration of the individual after death, and it sees God as a supernatural person, wholly independent of the finite, natural world; Whiteheadian process theism often rejects the continued self-conscious existence of the individual after death in favor of "objective immortality" in the consequent nature of God, and its God is a limited, albeit self-originating, deity rather than an omnipotent supreme being; feminist theologians such as Ruether and Christ discourage the interest in life after death altogether, and their deity is not a transcendent individual nor even self-originating, but a reality that human beings enact.

The underlying logic of feminist theology leads to the conclusion that human beings enact Goddess; the radical pragmatism embraced by many feminist theologians entails an enactment theology; and the emphasis on immanence so evident in feminist religious thought is supportive of the enactment model. There is but one piece of the puzzle remaining to be put in place, then: the centrality of relationship in feminist theology. In *Weaving the Visions*, Plaskow and Christ make clear that relationality is constitutive of human being for feminist theologians, and they note a connection between the feminist emphasis on relationality and that on divine immanence: the authors whom their collection anthologizes "agree that the self is essentially relational, inseparable from the limiting and enriching contexts of body, feeling, relationship, community, history and the web of life. The notion of the relational self can be correlated with the immanental turn in feminist views of the sacred: in both cases connection to that which is finite, changing, and limited is affirmed."[42] The grace of God "always comes to us in, with, and through each other," as Beverly Harrison puts it.[43] Taking this to its logical conclusion, Sharon Welch writes, "the divine *is* . . . relational power, and . . . it is neither necessary nor liberatory to posit a substance or ground that exists outside of relational power."[44]

In order to illustrate how all of the pieces fit together here, let us read Ruether's *Sexism and God-Talk* as an example of the enactment model of deity. First, note Ruether's claim that God/ess is experienced "in and through relationships, healing our broken relations with our bodies, with other people, with nature."[45] According to Ruether, it is when we overcome the destructive mindset of man vs. woman, rich vs. poor, and spirit vs. nature—dualisms that separate us from nature and from other human beings—that we find ourselves in relation to divinity: "Community with God/ess exists precisely in and through this renewed community of creation."[46]

The components of the relationship that Ruether is describing here are the self, other persons, and nature. Nature should be taken to mean not just the individual plants, animals, and other entities that make up the natural order, but also the force that animates all of nature, what other feminist thinkers such as Christ and Daly frequently call the "power of being." The expression "power of being" is sufficiently ambiguous to admit of several interpretations. Of course it does have a Tillichian resonance, and in Tillich's theology it involves a dialectical negation of the finite: finitude is the limitation or negation of being by nonbeing, while the power of being (or "being-itself") negates the negation of being.[47] But given feminist theology's commitment to nature and the finite, it is more plausible to read "power of being" not in Tillich's terms as something beyond the finite, but as the animating force that flows through every natural entity.[48]

None of the constituent elements of the relation Ruether describes has, considered by itself, the qualities of deity, not even her version of the undergirding power that manifests itself in nature. By itself, this power is only the "cosmic matrix of matter/energy."[49] This is hardly the stuff of ultimate concern, i.e., of religious passion and devotion. The cosmic matrix of matter/energy, while obviously the basis of our existence, is at best indifferent to the fulfillment of the human project or the future of any other species. It is perfectly possible, for example, that a huge meteor may someday slam into Earth and propel so much dust and debris into the atmosphere that all life here will be obliterated. This would be totally consistent with the so-called laws of nature, the principles that obtain within the cosmic matrix. And it would make no difference to the cosmic matrix if this calamity were to occur just as oppressed peoples were first finding their voices.

The cosmic matrix of matter/energy is not God/ess, then, but it is a crucial element in the being of God/ess. For God/ess appears when one relates to the cosmic matrix, and the beings that it undergirds, in a particular fashion. When I recognize that I am not all, that I am only a small part of the encompassing cosmic matrix, that I am finite and must die, then I may also recognize that I cannot set myself up in a position of dominance over other beings. I may come to accept the limitations of my own being and my responsibilities toward other beings, both human and nonhuman. And this relation to the cosmic matrix and the beings that it grounds enacts the divine. God/ess appears as this salvific relation, as this "renewed community of creation." Buber's philosophy of the self comes into play here, for while "I" must in some sense decide to engage in this relationship, the character of the "I" is determined by the relation itself. The relation empowers a new way of being for the "I."

The difference between the undergirding power of nature considered by itself and the larger religious relation of which it is an essential, catalytic element is nicely, if unintentionally, suggested by the contrast between Ruether's two expressions, "cosmic matrix of matter/energy" and "Primal Matrix." While the former suggests a dispassionate, even technical attitude, the latter has a poetic resonance. Again, while the word "matrix" in "cosmic matrix of matter/energy" is at least quasi-scientific, when it is capitalized and juxtaposed with "primal," it much more readily displays its original meaning of womb and its etymological connection with the word "mother."[50]

It is important to note the interplay of transcendence and immanence here. Because God/ess is a relation that we enact, divine being is radically immanent. But because there are constituent elements of this relation that transcend us—the matrix of nature, or power of being, and all of the beings that it undergirds—and because the relation itself taken as a whole is infinitely more than our own being and sustains us in a new and more productive way of being even as we enact it, the divine is also transcendent. Insofar as the cosmic matrix or power of being is one of the constituent elements of the relation that is God/ess, we can say that God/ess is the source of our existence and that she maintains us in existence. And the larger relation is a source of meaning and a focus of commitment, so that it is also possible to say that God/ess is the source and sustainer of our being in that fuller sense that includes our consciousness of purpose.

The same reading can be made of Ruether's later book, *Gaia and God: An Ecofeminist Theology of Earth Healing*. "To believe in divine being," she tells us, means to believe that the qualities of consciousness and altruism that we find in the human species "are rooted in and respond to the life power from which the universe itself arises."[51] But are these qualities rooted in that undergirding life power in the way in which a Thomistic effect is rooted in its cause, so that the effect can possess only those qualities already found in the cause? Or is it through the relationship between the human species and the underlying life power that these qualities first come into being? If we assume that Ruether would choose the latter option, since it is consistent with the contemporary world view, then it appears that the power of life is not itself divine; what is divine is the relation that is enacted between human beings and the power of life.

Other feminist theologies exhibit a similar pattern. Mary Daly, for instance, often appears simply to equate the divine with the "power of being."[52] But her intention is probably more clearly expressed in her claim that the Goddess is "the Self-affirming be-ing of women."[53] This suggests that divinity is not to be identified with the power of being but, rather, with a particular way in which women can tap into the power of being in themselves and make it productive of a new feminist consciousness and mode of existence. Women enact divinity in themselves through a particular relation to the power of being.

In a similar fashion, Carol Christ focuses on nature in her own "journey to the Goddess," but not nature by itself. She explains that "Goddess symbolism unites two themes in my work: she is woman and she is nature."[54] That is, Goddess is not to be equated with nature, but understood as a special kind of relation that can obtain between women and nature. The Goddess is born when women come to understand their rootedness in nature and finitude, and claim that power that such rootedness confers. This is, says Christ, "a deeply relational power, which comes from understanding the connection of my power of being to that of all other life."[55]

The *telos* of all of these radically relational theologies—what I have named the enactment model of deity— is succinctly expressed in Dorothee Sölle's observation that "today, the dispute over whether God can be thought of beyond us as resting in himself and unrelated, or whether God is the relationship itself and can be thought of only as relationship, seems to me to be one of the most important arguments between male-patriarchal and feminist theology."[56]

The enactment model gives us a particularly clear picture of the transformation of God. The notion of God as supernatural personal agent is abandoned here, as are numerous other attributes of the traditional God of Judaism and Christianity. No one will deny, I think, that this model represents a radical departure from previous ideas of

God, especially on ontological issues. But a strong case can be made for the claim that the enactment model of deity preserves those essential elements of the notion of God that traditional theism no longer can.

There can be little doubt that the feminist theologies interpreted here in terms of the enactment model escape conceptual privatization. First of all, these theologies are motivated by a concern that automatically places the self within the larger spheres of society and history. They are concerned to free women from bondage to patriarchal forces that have bedeviled them through the ages, forces brought to bear in social, political, and economic practice. In fact, it is on this field of struggle that Goddess is enacted: the social, political, and economic realms—which taken together constitute the realm of history—provide the context in which deity comes to be.

Of course, it may happen that roughly the same understanding of the human responsibility for history found in a feminist enactment theology can also result from some variation of traditional theism. In Kathryn Tanner's careful and impressive book, *The Politics of God*, for example, one sees something close to traditional theism connected with a passionate concern for progressive human action in the social and political arenas.[57] But whereas concern for social justice is a systemic feature of a feminist enactment theology, it is only an optional feature of traditional theism. And, once again, even in those contemporary versions of traditional theism that have a strong commitment to *human* action in the public sphere, it is unclear that one can make sense of the claim that *God* is active outside the private domain.[58] By contrast, the enacted Goddess is, as we have seen, embodied precisely in history.[59]

The feminist theologies under consideration here escape conceptual privatization, secondly, because they do not cede the world of nature to nonreligious sensibilities. On the contrary, nature, along with the power of being manifested in it, is understood as one of the constituent elements of the relation through which the divine is enacted. As a result, these theologies issue in a piety that celebrates nature, that regards it as in some sense sacred, and that recaptures it for the divine.[60]

It thus appears that both the negative moment—the abandonment of God as supernatural personal agent—and the positive moment—the reclaiming of extra-personal dimensions of reality for divine influence—that are necessary to break free from conceptual privatization are present in these enactment theologies. And, in fact, it is possible to show that all of the essential elements of the notion of God are protected here. Recall that, according to our earlier definition, God is to be understood as the transcendent source of life and meaning that ultimately informs the believer's every thought and action. The feminists' God or Goddess is a source of life, especially insofar as she includes nature and what undergirds it, what Ruether calls the "cosmic matrix of matter/energy." Ruether's God/ess is the divine womb, the "life power from which the universe itself arises."[61] Meaning too surely flows from the divine as understood in the feminist theologies surveyed above. In fact the relation that is Goddess is an encompassing framework within which one's whole life and being are to be understood. And we have already seen that the divine conceived in this way informs not just the private sphere, but the wider dimensions of reality in which human beings find themselves as well.

There is a clear sense, too, in which enactment piety is monotheistic. The relation that is Goddess is one. A relation can be made up of a complex of elements, but precisely as *a* relation, the relationship itself is a unity. And in the case of the relation that is Goddess, even the individual elements of the relationship bespeak wholeness. First of all, it is a relation to the one human community, not just to isolated pockets of humanity, even if we never concretely encounter more than a miniscule part of that larger human community. Second, it is a relation to the one power of being or cosmic matrix of matter/energy. And, thirdly, it is a relation to nature, which, however multiform, is ultimately one, a fact graphically demonstrated by the ecological crisis: we in the industrialized world cannot assume, for example, that our destruction of the ozone layer is our concern alone, for the world of nature is a continuous whole, and such destruction can affect beings on every portion of the planet.

This is not to say that there is no multiplicity in enactment piety. On the contrary, there are inumerable points of entry into the relation that is Goddess; each person who chooses to enact the relation does so from his or her own unique situation and perspective. And, as we shall discover later on, the symbols that can be used to make the enacted Goddess concretely present to consciousness can be many and diverse in a way not true for traditional theism. Enactment religiosity is best described, then, as a radically polysymbolic monotheism.[62]

The one component of our definition of God that probably needs further analysis, at least where the enactment model is concerned, is transcendence. Thus far we have noted that genuine transcendence, far from excluding immanence, is dependent upon it.[63] As a result, we have no reason for supposing that the emphasis on immanence in feminist theology excludes transcendence. Indeed we have found important examples of transcendence in the enactment model of Goddess: the constituent elements of the relation in which Goddess is enacted, and especially that relation itself, clearly transcend the human. But down through the centuries in Western history the concept of transcendence has been closely associated with the wholly other supreme being of traditional theism, who is eternal and omnipotent, and who freely created the world out of nothing. Thus, the claim that the enacted deity is genuinely transcendent needs further defense.

Note, first of all, that the objection according to which the enactment model is flawed because it does not include the kind of transcendence connected with the more traditional concept of God, seems to presuppose that the God of traditional theism exists, or at least that the attempt to conceive of God in that traditional fashion is viable. But if the concept of a supernatural personal agent breaks down in the contemporary world and undermines the essence of the notion of God, we are hardly in a position to hold up this traditional concept of God as a criterion. In other words, the fact that the enactment model of Goddess does not include exactly the same sort of transcendence that is associated with the model of God as supernatural personal agent does not undermine the former model, considering the fact that the latter is in a state of crisis. Of course it is necessary that the enacted Goddess manifest something that bears at least a strong family resemblance to what has been meant by "transcendence" in the past; otherwise the term "transcendence" ought not to be used at all. But we have already seen that there are significant ways in which the enacted Goddess sustains and exceeds the human individual, and these ways do bear a definite resemblance to what has been meant by "transcendence" in previous epochs.

Second, suppose that we take a more practical approach to transcendence. That is, instead of thinking of transcendence as applying directly to attributes of deity, let us consider the ways in which *concepts* of God can transcend those who create them. It is a notorious fact that the traditional notion of God as Supreme Being has proved sufficiently malleable to serve almost every conceivable human goal. God as supernatural personal agent has been invoked by warring nations to bring victory against one another; he has served as a source of assurance that the war in which one is engaged is a righteous cause; he is used to prop up the current social order and condemn those who would try to change it; he can be understood as requiring one to overthrow the present order; sometimes he is even supposed to help one sell more vacuum cleaners or win a baseball game. In short, this traditional idea of God, while it attributes a powerful form of transcendence to the reality it purports to describe, seems to possess no transcendence whatsoever *as a concept*. When judged by its ability to resist attempts by its creators to use it for their own selfish, all-too-human interests, it resembles the proverbial wax nose that any knave can mold to suit his or her own face.

One might counter that the feminist enactment theology that I have outlined here is hardly pure in this regard either. Surely it serves a particular social and political agenda. In fact I have argued that it is precisely this that most clearly shows that it escapes conceptual privatization. What is significantly different about this enactment theology, though, is that it seems to possess at least some built-in limits against manipulation. Because it is constructed around relation with other human beings and with nature, it is necessarily limited by the needs of others, meaning both other human beings and nature as other. The traditional model of God wants to talk of God as radically other, but how this otherness is conceived is up to the persons using the model; God's otherness is, paradoxically, at the disposal of the believer. In the enactment model, by contrast, the otherness of deity is protected by the concrete reality of otherness found in other persons and in nature. Of course, this is still a matter of the individual's *interpretation* of that otherness. But even though it must be filtered through one's own reading of the world, the otherness of persons and nature is an insistent presence that cannot easily be denied. As we noted earlier, for example, I cannot simply choose what I want to think about nature: gravity will have its way despite my wishes. Practically speaking, then, the enactment model of the divine seems to manifest a strikingly greater degree of transcendence than the model of God as Supreme Being.

This second observation on behalf of the transcendent character of the enacted Goddess leads to a third consideration: it is essentially a moral force that lies behind the enactment of Goddess. One responds to the imperative represented by the otherness of other persons, the world of nature, and that power of being that allows things to exist. The relation that is Goddess is a matter of recognizing one's proper place in the overarching scheme of things, one's responsibilities, limitations, and possibilities vis-à-vis the larger community of reality. If Goddess is to be understood, then, in terms of the moral imperative, perhaps we should conclude that Goddess is, in Emmanuel Levinas' phrase, "otherwise than being."[64]

Levinas' radical philosophy is just one of the approaches to ethics that can be pursued in an enactment theology. But its extreme interpretation of transcendence makes it a particularly useful example for our purposes. The God of traditional theism is the most perfect being, the greatest of all things that exist. But as a being, albeit the Supreme Being, this God is still less than being-itself. Thus, God conceived as being-itself transcends the God of the "onto-theological" tradition, God conceived as the greatest possible being.[65] But the God (or the Goddess) of the moral imperative transcends even God as being-itself, for whereas the thinking of being is a function of the unity of the horizon of consciousness (i.e., to think about being is to think an ultimate unity, a unity that is finally dependent on the unity of consciousness), the moral imperative stands outside that horizon: it is, in terms of Levinas' thought, an infinite demand that no horizon can encompass and, as such, always anterior to the "now" of consciousness. The moral imperative is infinite, in that I am never done with my duty to my neighbor. Thus, the God of the moral imperative is a truly infinite God, a radically transcendent deity.

Yet another consideration on behalf of the transcendent character of the enacted Goddess has to do with the element of mystery. That which is mysterious transcends, by definition, our ability to conceptually plumb it. But surely there is something radically mysterious about the encounter with the other, beginning with the human other. I can never really know another person; something of his or her being always remains opaque to me. After all, contemporary philosophies of selfhood suggest that I can never make even my own subjectivity fully transparent to myself. And the power of being, another constituent element of the relation that enacts Goddess, is also mysterious. It is a force in which I and all other parts of nature participate immediately, rather than a conceptualizable structure or entity. Hence, it is better expressed in symbol or ritual than in philosophical prose. Consider, as an example, the following song from the Gabon Pygmys of Africa, which exemplifies much the same sense of the power of being that is found in many works of feminist religious thought:

The fish does . . . HIP
The bird does . . . VISS
The marmot does . . . GNAN

I throw myself to the left,
I turn myself to the right,
I act the fish,
Which darts in the water, which darts
Which twists about, which leaps—
All lives, all dances, and all is loud.

The fish does . . . HIP
The bird does . . . VISS
The marmot does . . . GNAN
The bird flies away,
It flies, flies, flies,
Goes, returns, passes,

Climbs, soars and drops.
I act the bird—
All lives, all dances, and all is loud.

The fish does . . . HIP
The bird does . . . VISS
The marmot does . . . GNAN

The monkey from branch to branch,
Runs, bounds and leaps,
With his wife, with his brat,
His mouth full, his tail in the air,
There goes the monkey! There goes the monkey!
All lives, all dances, and all is loud.[66]

There is something about the power of being that makes a symbolic or ritual approach to it much more effective than an (allegedly) literal, philosophical analysis.

We have considered a number of reasons for holding that the enacted deity is genuinely transcendent. It would appear, then, that all of the pieces of the puzzle are in place: this Goddess is not only the source of life and meaning that informs all of the believer's thinking and action, she is also transcendent. Thus, we are in a position to say that in this current of feminist theology, the idea of God as personal agent has been abandoned and the essential core or identity of the concept of God has been preserved. In short, God has been transformed.

This is, of course, but one example of how the sacred might be, or is being, transformed. There may be other ways to work out an enactment theology in addition to the path taken by this species of feminist religious thought. Furthermore, there may be ways to transform God that do not involve enactment at all. The transformation process is not a matter of some ineluctable telos. Rather, it begins with accidental historical juxtapositions, as when contemporary communication technologies collide with traditional theistic approaches to the problem of theodicy. The attempt to preserve the essentials of the notion of God in the face of this sort of challenge may proceed according to the inner logic of that notion, yet even here there is no metaphysically necessary telos at work. The current of feminist theology we have been exploring has the significant virtue of providing a clear example of the transformation of the divine; how it will relate to other versions of transformation cannot be predicted at this historical juncture.

❖ IV ❖

Layers of Continuity and Change

*G*od is the core of Western religiosity. Of course, the metaphor of the core implies that while God is at the center of religion, there are other important elements making up the phenomenon of religion too. That is, as we ordinarily use the word "religion" in the West, we take it to refer not only to God but also to numerous other matters directly and indirectly connected with God. Obviously, just which other matters are included in our sense of religion can vary; that is what one ought to expect from a family resemblance concept such as religion. But suffice it to say that, if the core of religion is transformed, there are going to be changes in the outer layers of the phenomenon of religion as well. It is only when we have examined some of these changes that we can fully understand what is involved in the transformation of religion.

Suppose that God is transformed in the manner suggested by the enactment model of the divine. What else changes along with the concept of God? There will be important changes, I think, in each of the following: the notion of the self in its relation to the divine; the sense in which religion can be understood as ultimate concern; the phenomenon of religious experience; the practice of worship; and the way in which religion addresses the dilemmas that result from human finitude. The task before us is to determine the extent to which these changes are true departures from traditional piety, and the extent to which they remain continuous with tradition in spite of change.

Up to this point, we have confined our attention to continuity and change in the *content* of religion; we have defined religion in terms of its substance: for Western religion, belief in God. But now that we are turning to some of the outer layers of God-centered religiosity, we shall have occasion to examine functional dimensions of religion as well.

It is important to keep in mind that, in principle, there can be many variations on the basic notion of enacting the divine. I have used feminist theology as one example, and even within the confines of feminist theology I have had to abstract from the unique characteristics of particular feminist positions; my approach has been to construct something like an ideal type of enactment theology on the basis of some common themes in various feminist religious thinkers. Thus, not everything said below about the manifold layers of continuity and change will apply to every possible version of enactment theology. At least in some cases, though—those in which what is at issue are basic, systemic characteristics of the enactment model of God—it ought to be possible to make statements that will apply to all variations of the enactment model. The discussions of the relation of the self to God and of religion as ultimate concern fall in this category, I think. In other cases, however, where the characteristics of particular versions of enactment theology become relevant—e.g., in the discussions of religious experience, worship and ritual, and the function of religion over against the dilemmas inherent in finitude—we shall have to be satisfied with considering the implications of that feminist variation on the enactment approach that is outlined above.

We begin with the *the self in its relation to God.* Classical Christian thinkers often conceive of all entities as essentially artifacts of the divine: In that all things are created by God, they all have their essence determined by the purpose that God had in mind when he made them. The idea that human beings in particular should be understood as divine artifacts is nowhere better or more famously articulated than in the words of Augustine: "Thou hast formed us for Thyself, and our hearts are restless until they find rest in Thee."[1] A parallel formulation is found in the contemporary Jewish thinker Leo Baeck, who explains that "in religion life finds its natural growth from the soil in which it was created and toward the end for which it was formed. In religion man attains his true self. . . ."[2]

In enactment theology, in contrast, Goddess may empower new ways of life, but she is not a supernatural agent who created human beings as artifacts. Consider what this means for understanding the destiny of the human self and the possibility of salvation: In the classical model, one knows that a thorough-going happiness is possible for human beings, if not in this life then in the next, since God has created us with that possibility at the very center of our being. We need only put ourselves in proper relation to God for the possibility to be actualized. But viewed from the perspective of the enactment model of God, we are accidental products of natural processes and have no *telos* built into our being. We experience various kinds of happiness; if we are fortunate, we may be happy more of the time than unhappy. But we have no reason to think that there is any possibility of perfect happiness and fulfillment, or of a happiness that encompasses every dimension of our being, for we are not artifacts destined for any such ultimate and supernatural beatitude. Perhaps, then, the very notion of salvation, so central to traditional religious consiousness, now becomes a heuristic symbol rather than a concept pointing to a literal state of existence.

The same matter can be put in slightly different terms: Christian analyses of selfhood have always acknowledged, indeed even emphasized, the conflicted character of the *fallen* self. But the loss of the artifact relation (in which God is creator and human beings creature), along with Freudian and more recent attempts to de-unify or de-center our picture of the self, results in a conception of the self as *essentially* conflicted. This is, paradoxically, tantamount to conceiving the self as a kind of non-essence.

Some of the changes attendant on a transformation of the sacred may be radical. The abandonment of the notion of God as supernatural personal agent is one example, but the change now before us may be equally significant. For we are really saying that there may be no such thing as "salvation" or "enlightenment" in the traditional senses of those terms. Perhaps neither a final, unshakable happiness nor a thorough-going change of our way of existence is within our grasp. Perhaps religion can no longer be described, in Frederick Streng's formulation, as a matter of "ultimate transformation."[3] It may be that the religious quest must now soberly be acknowledged as a search for a relative kind of fulfillment and a partial *metanoia*, rather than for something absolute.

This acceptance of something less than an absolute solution to the challenges that inspire the religious quest is probably nowhere more tellingly displayed than in the approach to death implied by enactment theologies. As noted in the previous chapter, especially by reference to the work of Carol Christ and Rosemary Radford Ruether, an enacted deity—indeed any form of the divine that is rooted in the finite world—cannot be expected to give us any literal escape from death. We have no reason to think that individual consciousness can survive the demise of the body.

But an enactment theology does not therefore reduce us to nihilistic resignation in the face of death; it offers a genuinely religious response to death. From the perspective of the theologies (or thealogies) of Ruether and Christ, we ought to be able to abandon our egotistical resistance to death by recognizing our place in the larger scheme of things, i.e., by enacting the proper relationship with the power of being, nature, and other persons. We would then grasp the fact that death is one of the most natural of all phenomena, and that to resist death would be a denial of our finitude and a failure to recognize how the meaning of our being is given by our participation in something beyond ourselves.

Lest this seem such a radical change from previous religious practice that one suspects it of being no longer religious at all, it is important to remember that there are traditional religious analogues for it. For example, there is no firm evidence of belief in anything like heaven in the whole of the Hebrew Bible. In the period of Jewish history that it represents, one was more likely to face death by understanding oneself as rooted in a people and a covenant that transcended the death of the individual, and by having children to carry on one's particular line. (The concept of resurrection successfully entered Jewish piety only later, with the triumph of the Pharisees.) Death is not approached in the Hebrew Bible with total equanimity; life is much to be preferred to whatever comes after it. The Hebrew Bible then offers some solace in the face of death and important religious resources for confronting it, but there is no suggestion of a perfect and happy solution to our anxiety before the thought of having to die. Similarly, the enactment model of deity and the piety it inspires ought to offer a significant religious response to the anxiety of death, but no perfect transcendence of it.

It is difficult to overestimate the importance of this shift in piety from the expectation of total fulfillment and transformation to something that is partial and ambiguous. If we once again briefly turn our attention to that instructive critic of religion, Sigmund Freud, we find that an important part of Freud's attack on religion as mere wishful thinking is his contention that religion is a form of psychological immaturity. Religion is childish, and the desire for God is nothing more than the wish for a cosmic father to look after us. Freud thus sees his attack as effecting "education to reality."[4] The transformation of piety represented by devotion to an enacted deity, which is concretely represented in the approach to death taken by Ruether and Christ, appears relatively immune from Freud's assault. This is a piety that, by its very nature, accepts limitation and imperfection. It is a piety of resignation, not of a despairing sort, but of the kind that issues in a mature confrontation with our finitude. Here we encounter genuine transcendence, but we also accept the fact that our fulfillment and the transformation of our lives will be consonant with what we are: we are products of nature, or perhaps of something that we might call the "power of being" or the "cosmic matrix of matter/energy"; we are not divine artifacts, destined for eternal bliss and righteousness.

As a second instance of difference from more traditional piety, a difference that is again related to the loss of the artifact relation between God and human being, consider *the reconfiguration of "ultimate concern."* That definition of religion was authored in the twentieth century by Paul Tillich, as has already been noted. But "ultimate concern" is Tillich's influential attempt to provide an "abstract translation of the Great Commandment" taught by Jesus, which is derived from the Hebrew Bible: "Here, O Israel: The Lord is our God, the Lord alone. You shall love the Lord your God with all your heart, and with all your soul, and with all your might."[5] In short, true religion consists in making God one's ultimate concern.

Let us begin to unpack what is at issue here by distinguishing between the material and the formal role of God in traditional theistic piety. By the material role, I mean God adored for his own sake; by the formal role, I mean devotion to God as a guide for relating to other entities and organizing our behavior in the world. In traditional theism, at least of the Christian variety, wherein human beings are understood as divine artifacts, the material role of God in piety *includes* the formal role. That is, to love and worship God is automatically to be put in the proper relationship to all other things and to correctly discharge all other responsibilities. It is part of our character as artifacts, created to devote ourselves to God, that when we focus all our attention upon God, everything will be in order. If we return to Augustine's thought, for example, we find that his perspective can be summarized in the advice, "Love God and do as you please."[6] This should not be taken to mean that the only thing that matters is loving God, i.e., that behavior in all other realms of life is simply without importance. Rather, what is intended here is the notion that if one loves God one will automatically behave rightly in all that one does, for to love God is to find the end for which one has been created and the place that one is meant to occupy in the larger scheme of creation. Love of God orients the will in such a way that what one pleases to do will always be the right course of action. The artifact relation between God and human beings implies that devotion to God is, by itself, both a necessary and a sufficient condition for human fulfillment and virtuous behavior. Thus, the pious Christian can look to the God who appears in Christ as his or her "*only* comfort, in life and in death," as the opening question of the *Heidelberg Catechism* would have it.[7] All else is contained within devotion to God.

By contrast, from the vantage point of the enactment model, the material role of Goddess does not encompass Goddess's formal role. Indeed, here the formal role has priority, for Goddess only appears as one enters into relation with various other aspects of reality. In this case, we cannot even make sense of the idea of focusing exclusively on Goddess: what would it mean to focus on Goddess apart from nature and other persons, for example, given that Goddess is a relation that the self enacts with nature and other persons (and with the power of being)? Here piety has shifted from a concentration on Goddess as somehow valuable in and of herself, to devotion to Goddess as a particular way of contextualizing one's existence. Inasmuch as a piety that enacts Goddess must do without the artifact relation between Goddess and human being and the resultant assumption that Goddess is the sufficient condition of human fulfillment, it appears that such a piety cannot be described in terms of ultimate concern.

But this appearance is deceptive, for there is still a sense in which the devotee of the enacted Goddess might refer to that Goddess as of unconditional concern. There can be no such thing as exclusive devotion to the enacted deity, and we cannot talk in this case about a material form of piety that encompasses a formal kind of piety. But insofar as Goddess herself is a relation that encompasses the rest of reality, concern about Goddess is simultaneously a concern about these other things and the proper relationship with them. Thus, one can talk about unconditional devotion to the enacted Goddess, not in the sense that one focuses on this Goddess as a separate entity and, through doing so, is automatically placed in the right relation with everything else, but in the sense that concern about this Goddess is by its very nature concern about all of the elements that make up the relation that is Goddess.[8] To put it slightly differently, while in traditional Christian theism, devotion to God automatically *results* in proper relation to all other things due to the fashion in which God has constructed us, in the enactment model devotion to God *is* proper relation to all other things.[9] It turns out that devotion to the enacted Goddess can still be a matter of ultimate concern. But ultimate concern has been transformed along with the God who is its object. Different deities, it seems, demand different kinds of piety.[10]

The first topic considered—the self in relation to God within the enactment model—involves a clear difference from more traditional forms of God-centered piety, with little or no continuity with those more traditional pieties. The second topic—religion as ultimate concern in the enactment model—involves equal parts of change and continuity. When we turn to a consideration of *religious experience* and the enacted Goddess, we encounter a change from theism in its contemporary, privatized mode, that actually results in a deeper continuity with the piety of previous centuries.

What is meant, first of all, by "religious experience"? It is a phrase that is frequently used, but not so frequently defined. We can follow Kant in holding that experience always involves more than just the mind's own activity. "Intuition," in the technical sense of the term, is required for experience: something must be *given* to the mind.[11] For Kant himself, the only source of such intuition is the senses; other philosophers, including the so-called post-Kantians, have held that thinking can also be intuitive. But whether one sides with Kant, with the post-Kantians, or with neither, it is safe to say that experience, by definition, *must* include the reception of something given to us, some kind of material or data that is given to the mind rather than being produced by it.

If we are to talk about religious experience, then, we must find a relation to religious objects that includes the element of givenness. And if what is sought by religion is nonmaterial, then it initially appears that there must exist some mode of givenness that does not directly depend upon the senses. Some such nonsensible mode of givenness is what is implied in the following passage from William James' classic study, *The Varieties of Religious Experience*: "It is as if there were in the human consciousness a *sense of reality, a feeling of objective presence, a perception* of what we may call 'something there,' more deep and more general than any of the special and particular 'senses' by which the current psychology supposes existent realities to be originally revealed."[12] The traditional theist will see religious experience of this sort as the gift of God. But what part of the mind is able to receive these supernatural impressions? Must we posit some special organ of reception? The theist can perhaps overcome this apparent difficulty by holding that God provides not only the content of the experience, but also the capacity with which to receive it. The receptive capacity too, in other words, is a supernatural gift. This will hardly satisfy the skeptic, of course. The skeptic will inevitably deem the sort of experience described by James as a purely subjective phenomenon: the religious person believes that he or she is experiencing the divine, but this belief cannot be credited, since we know of no faculty for receiving data from some transcendent, immaterial reality. The alleged religious experience cannot be distinguished from mere emotion. However, it must be granted that the theist's position is at least consistent. If one accepts the basic tenets of traditional theism, it makes sense to suppose that religious experiences are possible, in that God can supply both their content and the ability to receive that content.

One whose faith is invested in the enacted deity is obviously in a quite different position. This Goddess is not a supernatural agent and hence cannot address some special content to human consciousness and provide us with a supernatural faculty with which to intuit the content. But surely the enacted Goddess can be experienced. The feminist theologies or thealogies that we have taken as exemplary of the enactment approach are nothing if not experiential; this is contained within their emphasis on immanence. What is it to experience the enacted Goddess?

Of course one can have powerful experiences of some of the constituent elements of the relation that is Goddess: other persons and sundry parts of nature, for example, enter our experience in all sorts of ways. But we do not directly experience the totality of the human community, or nature as a whole.[13] Nor do we directly experience the relation itself, that immanent–transcendent reality that is Goddess. The enacted Goddess is not simply a matter of being put in an attitude of responsibility toward those concrete others that actually enter my experience. Rather, it means being put in an attitude of responsibility toward the whole "community of creation," to use a phrase of Ruether's that was cited earlier.[14] How, then, can we talk about religious experience in this context?

Here we must turn our attention to the role of symbol. A symbol stands in for what it symbolizes in order to make the symbolized concretely present. As Hans-Georg Gadamer observes, "A symbol not only points to something, but it represents, in that it takes the place of something. But to take the place of something means to make something present that is not present. . . . Only because the symbol presents in this way the presence of what it represents, is it treated with the reverance due to that which it symbolizes."[15]

Symbols have a crucial role to play in enactment piety. They can provide a concrete encounter with abstractions such as "nature" and the "human community". In fact, via symbolism we can concretely encounter the relation that is enacted to these things: i.e., Goddess.[16] There is an almost unlimited supply of candidates to symbolize the enacted deity. For example, since relation to the world of nature is such an important element in the being of this Goddess, all sorts of manifestations of nature might serve as symbols: trees, rocks, the ocean, animals—indeed many things that manifested the sacred in the most ancient religious traditions can all point to the divine now.

We get a clear sense here of the way in which a feminist enactment theology is a polysymbolic monotheism. As we noted in the previous chapter, enactment theology is monotheistic inasmuch as the enacted relation is one. But we now see that there are a multitude of symbols with which to concretize that relation, just as there are a multitude of vantage points from which different persons may decide to engage in the relation. The polysymbolism of enactment theology is different from what might be regarded as a polysymbolic element in traditional theism. In the latter case too, one can employ many different symbols to talk about God. But in traditional theism the symbols are not drawn from as many diverse contexts, and furthermore, manyness is only on the side of human perception. By contrast, where enactment theology is concerned, polysymbolism reflects a multiplicity within the being of Goddess herself. For while the enacted relation that is Goddess is indeed one, it has a genuine multiplicity of components. Difference exists within Goddess herself, not only among finite human attempts to grasp what Goddess is like. This difference comes from the uniqueness of the selves that decide to enact the relation, from their different experiences and convictions. And it comes from the almost infinite diversity of beings and entities within the one world of nature, which is such an important part of the relation that is Goddess. This explains why some might think of the sort of feminist piety that we have been investigating as a new polytheism. But the unity of the enacted relation suggests that this piety can more aptly be described as a radically polysymbolic monotheism.

The function of a symbol here is to stand in for the relation that is deity. And, given what was said above, this means that the symbol actually makes deity present for human consciousness.[17] Thus, I can have a concrete encounter with the divine through a tree, or the ocean, or a saintly person, for example. But are any of these encounters genuinely *experiential*? Is there an element of *givenness*? Some symbols surely do make the symbolized experientially present, because their symbolic material is derived from the physical world. Physical things—from rocks and trees to sound waves—can be given to the senses. If a particular tree is used as a symbol of the divine, then it is possible to experience the divine via the symbol that is its representative, indeed to experience it so powerfully that, as indicated in the quotation from Gadamer above, one responds to the tree with the awe one feels for the divinity that it symbolizes.[18]

Experiential symbols can also operate within the realm of the imagination. Jesus makes the Kingdom of God experientially present by describing the joy of a woman who finds a coin that had been lost.[19] I can see the woman in my imagination: her joy is expressed in her smile, her gestures, how she runs to tell her friends, i.e., in the kinds of physical phenomena to which the senses are attuned. Of course the woman's behavior is not actually given to my senses. Rather, at least on one reading of the imagination, I am creating her behavior in my mind, albeit guided by the words of Jesus' parable. The givenness involved here is an imaginary one, and it provides no basis for any claims about the actual existence of the woman and her joyous behavior. But imaginary experience is still a species of experience, and it is fully adequate for the operation of symbols: Jesus' parable can indeed allow the reader to experience the Kingdom through the representational behavior of the woman in his story.[19] Similarly, I can imagine some part of the natural world—perhaps a part that does not actually exist—and have it serve as an experiential symbol of Goddess.[20]

But is "Goddess" too a symbol? It seems to me that "Goddess" can play a variety of roles, including the symbolic. Sometimes "Goddess" functions simply as a proper name for the transcendent source of life and meaning that informs the believer's thought and action, as "God" did in traditional theism. But "Goddess" can also call to mind concrete images, such as the artistic representations of the goddesses by the ancient Greeks, or concrete manifestations of motherhood. Especially when connected with images of conception and giving birth, "Goddess" can in fact function as the paradigmatic symbol that embraces all others: everything that exists finds its source here.[21]

Thanks to experiential symbols, the devotee of the enacted God can just as legitimately speak of religious experience as can the devotee of the God of traditional theism. In fact, the former's religious experience is finally superior to the latter's, if we confine ourselves to the contemporary Western world, where the God of traditional theism is conceptually privatized. One who looks to *that* God will experience neither the thorough-going immanence nor the genuine transcendence worthy of deity.[22] Interestingly, then, the full-blown immanence and transcendence that can be experienced in the context of devotion to the enacted God parallels the religious experience of the Jewish and Christian traditions through the centuries, whereas religious experience available to one who embraces traditional theism in the contemporary West falls short of what was experienced in the past. The kind of radical changes effected by the enactment model of deity succeed, in other words, in preserving what has always been meant, in the West, by religious experience.

That the transformation of God represented by the enactment model makes possible anew the full-bodied religious experience of the past, suggests that the transformation process might be read as a *Destruktion* of traditional theism (in the sense that Heidegger employs the term *Destruktion*). In *Being and Time*, Heidegger wishes to carry out a *Destruktion* of the history of ontology. As Robert Scharlemann points out, to "destroy" in Heidegger's sense here "is not the same as to do away with; it is, rather, to analyze the elements of the structure of thought and trace them back to their beginning . . . in order to discover the experience that is at the basis of the structure."[23] One must recover that experience, because the later tradition of thought has obscured it. The enactment approach to the divine is a *Destruktion* of traditional theism, then, in that it recovers the kind of religious experience (though not necessarily the very same experience) that originally animated Western belief and devotion but that has been covered over by the privatized theism of the contemporary period.

It seems eminently clear that the enacted deity, as exemplified in feminist religious thought and behavior, affords her devotees a powerful kind of religious experience. This fact is important in evaluating the claim that the feminist positions we touched on in the previous chapter are genuinely religious, a claim that some might want to challenge. The challenge might go this way: the agendas that animate the projects of writers such as Mary Daly, Carol Christ, and Rosemary Radford Ruether do not in fact spring, at least in a straightforward way, from any religious tradition (including ancient Goddess religions). Rather, their concerns are obviously inspired by the great liberatory philosophies and movements of the modern West. It is impossible to imagine the work of Daly, Christ, and Ruether, in other words, without the background of the Enlightenment, modern liberal humanism, Marxism, and other currents of modern Western thought, even if contemporary feminism, religious feminism included, acts back upon some of these currents in such a way as to undermine them.[24] These emancipatory movements are not religious but secular; some of them have even tended to entail outright opposition to religion. Is it not the case, then, that the feminist "religious" agenda is really simply a secular agenda with only a patina of religion?[25] This conclusion seems only to be reinforced when one considers the fact that feminist religious thinkers cannot possibly see their agenda accomplished without cooperating with other segments of the feminist movement, segments that have no interest in religion whatsoever.

There is more than a grain of truth in this complaint, I think, and it applies not just to feminist religious movements, but to all contemporary emancipatory movements that claim to be motivated by religious sensibilities. Nonetheless, in the end it should be clear that, even if the social and political concerns at the heart of feminist theologies or thealogies have their origin in secular thought, feminist religious thinkers do more than simply cover these concerns with a thin layer of religion; they take the concerns up into a full-blown, genuinely religious universe of belief. As we have seen, these concerns are put in the context of devotion to a transcendent source of life and meaning that ultimately informs one's every thought and action. And now we can add that the religious feminist's social and political commitments are accompanied by a powerful kind of religious experience.

This discussion of the genuinely religious character of feminist enactment theologies, and by extension of other possible forms of enactment theology, leads to a consideration of *worship and ritual in the context of commitment to the enacted Goddess.* What continuities and changes exist here with respect to the religion of an earlier time? Let us start with the assumption that worship and religious ritual in the West have traditionally included at least the following elements: adoration of God; petition to God; communication with God; creation of a religious community; renewal of self and community; celebration; aesthetic expression; and instruction and learning.

With Nietzsche's warnings ringing in their ears, nineteenth- and twentieth-century Westerners may have the uncomfortable sense that glorifying a divinity denigrates the human condition. Yet adoration of God is at the center of traditional Western religious ritual; it is the very meaning of the term "worship." But how can one worship the enacted Goddess? Would not worship of this deity be idolatrous, since it is a deity that we have constructed? We begin to answer these questions by recalling that it is inaccurate to say that this Goddess is something human beings have constructed: human beings *enact* the relation that is Goddess, but both the various elements of the relation and the relation itself powerfully transcend the individuals who enact it. Of course the enacted Goddess is not a personal consciousness that demands worship, but there is no difficulty in imagining that the devotee of this Goddess will feel an awe before it that calls forth something akin to adoration. Furthermore, one cannot help but remember the words of the God of the prophet Isaiah here, a God who proclaims, "What to me is the multitude of your sacrifices? . . . bringing offerings is futile; incense is an abomination to me. . . . Learn to do good; seek justice, rescue the oppressed, defend the orphan, plead for the widow."[26] The feminist religious sensibility that serves as our model of the enactment approach to divinity certainly exemplifies the devotion demanded by Isaiah's God. There is, in other words, a strong element of continuity here, and much less change than one might initially suppose.

Change clearly triumphs, though, when we come to the element of petition. It is clear that traditional services of worship in the Jewish and Christian traditions do involve petition. This element is part of the most important prayer in Christianity, which requests that God "give us this day our daily bread." One cannot reasonably petition the enacted deity; there is no personal consciousness there to hear or respond. Of course the God of traditional theism is not as open to petition in the contemporary world as he once was: as conceptually privatized, God is no longer expected to respond to requests for intervention in the larger worlds of society, politics, and nature. But he can still be petitioned about matters that concern one's sense of self and one's behavior in the private sphere.

One might suppose that change will again outweigh continuity when it comes to a consideration of communication with God. For while this is obviously a part of traditional relgious ritual, one cannot communicate with the enacted deity. Once again, there is no personal consciousness there with which to interact. But surely a large part of what is sought in communication with God is a sense of participation in the divine, a sense that one does not stand apart from God but is taken up into the divine life and purpose. And this *is* a possible function of religious observance for the devotee of the enacted deity. One can easily imagine rituals that give the individual a sense of participating in the larger reality of the relation that is Goddess. Recall, in this regard, how symbols can make the enacted Goddess present to consciousness. Thus, the seeming inevitability of overwhelming change where communication with God is concerned turns out to be a misperception.

The other elements of worship and ritual, as they might be employed within an enactment piety, have even stronger and more obvious degrees of identity with traditional religious observance. Religious ritual within the context of an enactment religiosity will, for instance, clearly serve to reinforce a sense of community. The enacted deity is, after all, a matter of community among the self, other persons, nature, and the power of being. And there is every reason to expect that ritual will, in this context, serve as a vehicle of the renewal of the self and the community to which the self is committed. The renewal of the self might even include an element of reconciliation, a concept which is of central importance in traditional Christianity with its focus on fallenness and sin, and also plays a role in traditional Judaism, as evidenced in Yom Kippur. Celebration can certainly be a part of these rituals. Think, for instance, of how feminist theology points to a need for the celebration of women's abilities and experiences as they are understood in the context of our relation to the divine. This celebration, as well as most of the other elements of ritual, can take on powerful aesthetic dimensions. Feminist piety has already produced a wealth of poetic, plastic, and kinetic expression.[27] Finally, while worship focused on the enacted Goddess will not be as didactic as that found in traditional Christianity, with its strong doctrinal character, there is no reason to suppose that this worship cannot be a stimulus to reflection on the nature of the Goddess-relation and the way of existence that it entails. Let us say in summary, then, that religious ritual and worship centered on the enacted deity will involve notable differences from previous practice, but also surprising degrees of continuity.

We come, finally, to a consideration of continuity and change in *how the new piety and the old function vis-à-vis basic human anxieties.* This consideration too will reinforce the conclusion that the dynamic at work in the enactment approach to the divine is a genuinely religious one. If we return to Paul Tillich's functional definition of religion as ultimate concern, we find that "our ultimate concern is that which determines our being or not-being."[28] Ultimate concern is, in other words, tied up with the quest for being and the desire to overcome the threat of nonbeing. There is really nothing mysterious about the notion of nonbeing here, despite the convulsions it may induce in analytic philosophers. The threat of nonbeing is simply the negation of some aspect of my being, an experience of having some dimension of my life and its meaning undermined. Nonbeing is no *thing*, then, but rather the dissipation that human beings experience as part of the character of finite existence. Tillich has worked out the threat of nonbeing to which ultimate concern responds in terms of three fundamental types of anxiety.[29] That is, in good existentialist fashion, he understands these particular anxieties not as pathologies or as of merely subjective import, but as moods that disclose threats to our being. The threats, and the anxieties that accompany them, result from our finitude, and they have both a relative and an absolute form. They can be summed up as follows: we confront ontic anxiety, the relative form of which is the anxiety about fate, and the absolute form of which is the anxiety of death; moral anxiety includes the anxiety of guilt, which is a perception of a relative threat, and the anxiety of condemnation, which suggests an absolute threat to our moral being; and we must face spiritual anxiety, the relative form of which is the anxiety of emptiness, and whose absolute form is the anxiety of meaninglessness.

It is easy enough to imagine how the traditional theist's God helped to allay these anxieties. Let us take each anxiety in turn. The anxiety of fate is the disquieting, and potentially debilitating, awareness of how my existence is constricted by all sorts of circumstances and events beyond my control. It is, once again, a function of being finite, indeed part of the very meaning of finitude. But fate is only a relative threat; I still exist, in however limited a fashion. Death, by contrast is an absolute threat. The traditional theist can deal with fate, first of all, by giving up the hubris that would place the self at the center of the universe. The believer must "die to self" in the New Testament sense, and recognize that one's finite circumstances are part of one's creatureliness; only God is free of such limitations. The doctrine of providence helps here as well, for it suggests that the circumstances beyond my control are not beyond control altogether, that they are not meaningless, but that they are under the direction of a wise and benevolent deity. The anxiety of death is overcome, of course, in rabbinic Judaism and in Christianity, by the hope for eternal life with God in heaven.

The anxieties of guilt and condemnation register my sense that I have failed to discharge my moral responsibilities and have thereby undermined, or in the case of condemnation perhaps even destroyed, the moral core of my being. The Torah in Judaism and the teachings of Christ in Christianity clarify for the believer just what one's moral responsibilities are. But Tillich holds that all persons are subject to moral anxiety, no matter the tradition in which they find themselves. In other words, though ethical standards may vary greatly, nearly all human beings will at least occasionally encounter the gnawing sense that they are not living their lives as they ought to. The traditional Jewish theist can deal with this moral anxiety by trusting in God's willingness to forgive and the human capacity always to turn back to God, however badly one has done in the past. Traditional Christians will look to the atoning death of Christ and the whole notion of divine grace, whether conceived in Augustinian fashion as empowerment to live according to the divine dictates, or in Lutheran terms as forgiveness.

The traditional theist will of course look directly to God to overcome the anxieties of emptiness and meaninglessness. As we saw when we considered the artifact relation between God and human beings in traditional theism, human existence is seen as having a purpose and meaning built into it from the beginning, and that purpose and meaning is actualized by placing oneself in the proper relation to God.

What continuities and what differences come into play when we compare this traditional approach to the approach effected in an enactment piety? One difference is to be found in connection with the lack of the artifact relation between God and humanity, which we discussed above. As I emphasized there, because human being will no longer be thought of as an artifact with a telos that can be perfectly fulfilled by proper relation to the divine artificer, it is not reasonable to suppose that the anxieties can ever fully be overcome, even though the traditional theist might have been able to entertain such a hope.

Secondly, inasmuch as the anxieties are a consciousness of threats rooted in our finitude, the endeavor to escape the anxieties may be seen as an attempt to escape or transcend finitude. But advocates of an enactment theology may wish to evaluate the finite more positively than traditional theism has done. We saw this kind of positive evaluation in some of the feminist theologies that we touched on earlier. While enactment theologies will still address the anxieties of which Tillich speaks, they may have a different sense of what it means to deal successfully with them.

How will the practitioner of an enactment piety respond to the anxieties? No one answer can be given to this question, since different versions of the enactment approach to the divine may respond in quite different ways. In our consideration of enactment theology and the anxieties, we must simply attempt to illustrate the fact that an enactment theology can in principle address each anxiety, and we shall do this by imagining how an enactment theology might be crafted to do this. What is most important for our purposes, in other words, is not to show *how* a particular enactment theology will deal with the anxieties, but simply *that* enactment theologies can address the anxieties. This will reinforce the conclusion that, whatever their differences from more traditional pieties, enactment theologies are genuinely religious in character.

It will be useful to stay as close as possible to the kind of feminist enactment theology that has served as our paradigm up to this point. Where fate is concerned, a feminist thinker might want to make an important distinction. There is, on the one hand, something that we can designate natural fate: as part of the world of nature, we not only share the general limitations of the natural world, but also find ourselves dependent upon numerous particular segments of that world. This sort of fate is something that the feminist religious thinker will probably not wish to escape, especially if the thealogy of someone like Carol Christ is any guide. Part of what is meant here by religious awakening and piety is precisely a recognition and affirmation of one's rootedness in and dependence upon the world of nature. It is hard to miss the Taoistic flavor in this piety: the sacred manifests itself as the Way of the Universe, and to find the sacred is thus to harmonize oneself with this universe.

But historical fate is another matter. Historical fate is seldom inevitable, and what goes under the heading of historical fate is too often some form of oppression visited upon one group by another. The sort of feminist theology we are keeping in view will obviously see connectedness with the divine as a form of opposition to such oppression. The sense of community and relation that is Goddess is by its very nature the rejection of destructive and oppressive relationships.

We have touched on the response to death several times already. Death anxiety may be allayed by seeing it as part of our natural fate: death is part of the normal cycle of things; to attempt to avoid it is pure folly. Furthermore, the devotee of the enacted deity tends to look beyond the self to the larger relation in which the self is engaged, and that larger relation transcends the death of the individual.[30]

What about moral anxiety? Especially for a feminist version of enactment theology, there may be some reservations about traditional notions of sin, particularly as developed in Christianity. Feminists have often opposed the kind of self-denigrating focus on sin that they see as having been used to reinforce women's sense of inferiority and inadequacy. But feminist theologies are, nevertheless, animated by a moral concern, the concern to overturn the destructive forces of sexism and related forms of oppression. And if one cannot talk about a sense of guilt or condemnation of the traditional sort here, one can perhaps talk about the possibility of sin against one's own being, wherein one underestimates one's own dignity, and sin against the being of others, where "others" includes not just other persons but the world of nature as well. Feminist theologies like Rosemary Radford Ruether's respond to this sense of sin with the call to a thorough *metanoia* and the attempt to replace dualistic thinking, characterized by an "us versus them" mentality, with a relational mindset.[31] Furthermore, the very focus of enactment theology on relationship suggests the possibility of a particular kind of guilt and sin; namely, betrayal of that relationship and estrangement from the others who make up the relation. And this calls for some answer to moral anxiety, some possibility of reconciliation.[32]

As for spiritual anxiety, an enactment theology offers an overarching framework of meaning. The encompassing relation that is divinity provides something that all religions must provide, according to Clifford Geertz: namely, some conception of a "general order of existence."[33] Everything that we have seen so far about the enactment approach to God makes it clear that, as in more traditional religious sensibilities, this is a source of meaning for the religious person. Indeed, the enacted Goddess, it will be recalled, preserves the essence of the notion of God in that this deity is the transcendent source of life and meaning that informs the believer's every thought and action. To understand oneself as constantly in relation to other persons, nature, and the power of being is to have a powerful sense of purpose and worth: one is energized by responsibilities toward and connections with a multitude of others. The self possesses an undeniable dignity inasmuch as it plays an important role within the larger household of being. As we have seen, this role is not rewarded with bliss or perfection, but it is surely an antidote to the despair of meaninglessness.

The topics we have just surveyed—the nature of the self in relation to God; religion as ultimate concern; religious experience; ritual and worship; and the response to the anxieties that communicate fundamental threats to our being—suggest varying degrees of continuity and change between traditional piety and the piety that might characterize one's approach to an enacted Goddess. The matter of continuity is surely important here. In the case of religious experience, I have argued that the enacted Goddess has a more thorough-going identity with the piety of past centuries than does the God of traditional theism as that God exists in the contemporary period. And at other points too we discovered important continuities between an enactment religiosity and older pieties, so much so that there should be no hesitation in regarding enactment theology as a genuinely religious undertaking, and not just a political agenda clumsily disguised with a superficial religiosity. The enacted Goddess is continuous with the God of traditional Western religion, and her devotees can engage in forms of worship, enjoy religious experiences, and confront the fundamental anxieties of human existence in ways that are ultimately consistent with the spirit of traditional Western theistic faith.

But the element of change should by no means be underplayed either. It is necessary to confront the significant changes that our exploration has uncovered, in order to avoid any naive sense that one can rearrange the concept of deity without disturbing other dimensions of religion. These other dimensions must be disturbed, it seems, if the conception of God is transformed, and that fact points to an important question: While some type of transformation (the feminist one or another) may be necessary to preserve the essence of the notion of God, might some of the changes in the other layers of religion that follow in the wake of this transformation doom the transformed concept of the divine? One cannot rule out this possibility; surely it is conceivable that the very changes that are necessary to guarantee the integrity of the idea of God in the face of the contemporary form of the problem of theodicy will produce unintended changes in other layers of religion, and that these changes will prove inconsistent with particular psychological, social, or political exigencies and thus ultimately bring the transformed God to grief. Hence a question arises: What is the future of God? This question, if we engage it seriously, forces us to take a different approach to enactment theology from the one we have taken thus far. Up to this point, we have been considering an idealized form of enactment piety; we have, for the most part, simply accepted both its explicit and its implicit claims about what it can accomplish for its adherents.[33] But now we must cast a more skeptical eye on at least some of these claims.

❧ V ☙

The Future of God

When placed in the context of contemporary Western society, traditional theism destroys the essence of the notion of God. Suppose that the enactment model of God, or something very much like it, is the only alternative to traditional theism that preserves that essence. Of course it is unlikely that this is in fact the case; there are probably several different routes that belief in God can follow after the traditional pathway has been blocked. But it is a useful thought-experiment to imagine that the enactment model is the sole idea of God available to replace traditional theism, for this not only brings the contours of the issue of God's future into sharper relief, it also renders the exploration of this issue more manageable. To attempt to imagine the course of a whole host of God-ideas as they interact with innumerable social and cultural forces, as well as with one another, is an invitation to despair.[1] Even when we confine ourselves to a single model of God, the question about the future of God confronts us with so many variables that we must be resigned to mere conjecture, though we can hope that such conjecture is careful and well informed.

If we do bracket other alternatives, and imagine that the future of God rests with something like the enactment model, what do we discover? Any attempt to answer this question necessarily involves speculation about whether the enacted Goddess will be attractive or unattractive to persons, and it should be acknowledged from the outset that such speculation is, at least by some measures, idle. The human psyche is frequently opaque to our attempts to predict its inclinations. Furthermore, the psyche is always located in a complex and ever-changing social and cultural environment. In short, we cannot possibly *know* whether something like the enacted Goddess will, at a future date, prove sufficiently attractive to large numbers of persons for them to embrace it as an ultimate concern. But perhaps it is possible to hazard some educated guesses.

Let us begin with a number of negative considerations. First of all, it is quite clear that, even from the perspective of an enactment theology itself, there is no necessity about the enacted Goddess. That is, no one is compelled to engage in the relation that enacts the divine. I have underscored the point that the enactment model disavows any artifact relation between Goddess and humanity. Thus, human beings have no innate telos directing them to this Goddess. The advocate of the enacted deity must acknowledge, in other words, that other persons simply may not be interested in this Goddess, a fact that does not bode well for the future of the enacted divinity.

Indeed, it is not just a matter of there being no telos implanted in human nature to point us necessarily toward this Goddess. The advocate of the enacted Goddess cannot even claim that his or her notion of Goddess is a description of something that is undeniably real. In order to clarify this, let us imagine a different situation: we can imagine a theological scenario in which one holds that, while there is no inherent telos in human nature that aims at the God described in this theology, this God nevertheless exists. Hence, one could argue that although there may be no necessity of embracing God in order to find one's intended fulfillment as a human being, it is necessary to acknowledge God if one wants to understand the truth about the universe and what exists. But the devotee of the enacted Goddess cannot claim even this sort of necessity for his or her belief, for the enacted Goddess is only something that *can* be real, not something that is an inescapable part of reality.

Furthermore, one might argue that, although the whole notion of enacting Goddess suggests an immanent and practical approach to piety, an enactment piety is really only suited to a spiritual elite. After all, it is a piety that asks one to renounce many of the comforts of traditional theism, including the possibility of salvation as ordinarily understood. Isn't it possible that the vast majority of persons, offered the chance to embrace the enacted God or Goddess, may in effect say, "If this is what God is like, who needs her?" Harold Bloom's impish query seems apt here: "If medicine someday could grant immortality (virtually, to those who could pay for it), you, of course, still would be religious, but what about your neighbor?"[2] Or, to alter Bloom's question so that it exactly fits the circumstances we are considering: If it becomes clear that God cannot provide immortality, who will care about God?

Perhaps this can be pushed even further. Maybe it is the case that not even a spiritual elite, not even those who are capable of a large measure of resignation, can find sufficient meaning in the enacted Goddess. After all, while there is a lively feminist spirituality in this country, no unified tradition has yet developed around the specific sensibility that I am calling enactment piety. Thus, the only evidence of its effectiveness comes from the testimony of a few individuals (assuming that we are justified in taking the feminist thinkers discussed in the previous chapters as representatives of this piety). And this hardly makes for a reliable test, for when only a small number of individuals speaks to the power of a particular religious vision and lifestyle, we are not presented with enough instances to cancel out the possible influence of important variables. Suppose we take an individual's word for the fact that she or he has a meaningful life, one that allows for ethical sensitivity to others as well as an overall sense of well-being. The individual may attribute this happy state of affairs to his or her religious commitment, but how do we know that this is in fact its source? Perhaps this particular individual possesses a psychological makeup such that this approach to life is inevitable for her or him, regardless of what religious world view she or he embraces. Or perhaps this approach to life is the result of commitments other than the religious commitment, so that the individual is mistaken in attributing this power to his or her religious vision. Without the many instances and long periods of time represented by an established tradition, it is impossible to sort out these issues.

There is still another troubling matter to consider. Enactment piety appears to have no institutional bearers. That is, at least at present, there are no institutions, such as the Christian churches or Jewish synagogues, to represent this piety and provide it with a strong social base. Thus, it exists only within the minds of relatively isolated individuals. This is doubly problematic for something like a feminist enactment piety. First, if a piety has no institutional base, it will probably never develop the critical mass necessary to make it a viable mainstream religious option. But, secondly, given the very nature of feminist piety, with its commitment to dismantling sexism and other oppressive social forces, a feminist religiosity must have significant points of connection with the larger society so that it can influence that society. To speak of a "renewed community of creation" (Ruether) is to speak of something that can only be accomplished through action upon systemic elements of society. If, in this chapter, we are attempting to transcend the naiveté that threatens any talk about a relation characterized by justice and concern for the other, we have to recognize that many of the evils that would have to be eliminated in order to fully realize the Goddess-relation are social and economic, such as racism and poverty. One need hardly embrace a doctrinaire Marxism, for instance, to appreciate the degree to which the plight of the inner cities and their despairing minority communities is, in no small measure, a function of the development of capitalism, as Cornel West's prophetic Christianity reminds us.[3] A progressive religious vision, such as the one implied by a feminist enactment theology, seeks to influence these issues, but it cannot do so effectively if it has no social base.

One might respond by pointing out that there do exist various feminist communities in contemporary society that might become institutional bearers of enactment piety. This seems a rather insubstantial basis for hope, however. First, these feminist "communities" are only very loosely defined and organized; it is not yet clear how they will eventually fit into the larger institutional dynamics of Western society. Second, while we have taken certain feminist theologies as the most salient instances of what might be regarded as an enactment approach to God, we have also assumed that enactment piety need not be confined to feminist religious thought. Variations of the enactment approach to God that are not functions of a feminist consciousness can hardly look to feminist communities to provide an institutional base.[4]

But surely it is possible to find some positive indicators too. To begin with, a good portion of our argument in previous chapters has been to the effect that the enactment model of God is a true heir of the notion of God found in the Jewish and Christian religious traditions. The enactment model is an approach to God, though perhaps not the only approach, that preserves in the contemporary context the essence of the traditional notion of God. Hence, might it not be reasonable to hold that, even if the churches and synagogues are not at present institutional bearers of enactment piety, they may become so in the future? We must, after all, keep in mind the paradox of transformation, namely, that what appears on the surface to be a very different idea of God from the one held in previous centuries, actually represents a change in thinking that is required to preserve the essence of that traditional belief.

This train of thought affords a more optimistic reading, not only in that it provides enactment piety with institutional bearers, but also inasmuch as it suggests that, as a true heir of the traditional notion of God, the enactment model's future should be judged, at least in part, according to the inherent strengths of that traditional notion. In other words, suppose we hold that the enactment model of Goddess is what the traditional idea of God becomes when it enters the contemporary context. That idea has proved of inestimable value for millions of human beings over thousands of years.[5] Surely it is not unreasonable at least to entertain the hypothesis, then, that in its present permutation too, it can exercise a powerful, productive influence in human life.

On the other hand, there are no guarantees here. For one thing, even if the enactment approach to God is the genuine heir of the traditional God-idea, preserving what is in some sense definitive of the very notion of God, it may be that it is not those definitive characteristics that have made the idea of God existentially attractive through the ages. In order to clarify this possibility, let us assume that our description of God as "the transcendent source of life and meaning that ultimately influences the believer's every thought and action" does indeed get at the essence of the notion of God. It would follow that characteristics attributed to God other than those suggested by this description are not essential; they can be dropped without destroying the meaning of "God." But it may nonetheless be the case that it is some of the nonessential characteristics of God, qualities predicated of God through the bulk of the Jewish and Christian traditions even though they are not essential to God, that have made God most attractive to human beings. God does not have to be able to provide us with life after death in order to be God, but that ability is surely something that makes God useful and attractive to us.

Or, imagine something different: let us assume that the essential attributes of God, the qualities captured in our definition, *are* what have made God attractive through the ages. And let us assume, in addition, that the enactment model of Goddess preserves these essential attributes, in other words, that it is able to present these attributes anew in the contemporary environment. It may turn out, however, that the contemporary environment is sufficiently different from previous ages that these attributes are *no longer* attractive. Hence the observation that there is no guarantee that the enacted Goddess will prove attractive and productive to contemporary persons, even if she preserves the essential ingredients of a notion that has proved eminently attractive and productive in the past.

The task at hand, then, is to be specific. In other words, we must consider in specific terms just what the enacted Goddess can do that might make such a deity worth embracing, and thus assure her future. We already know that she cannot provide life after death or providentially order human history, but surely there must be some things that she can be credited with having the power to accomplish, even if we now intend to approach our investigation with a healthy dose of skepticism.

We start with the way in which the very notion of God, the enacted Goddess included, evokes a sense of selfhood for human beings. This is a sense of selfhood that is independent of any notion of the self as an artifact of the divine. In a fascinating meditation on the word "God," Karl Rahner asserts that "If the word 'God' really did not exist, then neither would these two things exist any more for man [*sic*], the single whole of reality as such and the single whole of human existence in the mutual interpenetration of both aspects."[6] Thus, "the absolute death of the word 'God,' including even the eradication of its past, would be the signal, no longer heard by anyone, that man [*sic*] himself had died."[7] Human beings would regress to the level of a "clever animal."[8] Rahner has in mind, I think, the fact that we come to a sense of the self and its wholeness by distinguishing the self from what is not self: I am not you, and I am not the other things that appear in my field of vision (or, more strongly, I *am* what is not you, and what is not any of the other things in my field of vision). Where, then, do I find the fullest perspective on the self? It may be, as Heidegger suggests, that thinking about my death is crucial, for it will allow me to think my existence as a whole and to differentiate it from what does not die with me.[9] But the most encompassing perspective will be afforded by situating the self within the whole of reality: the self is most fully understood in its unique selfhood when it stands out against everything else that is, and against the ultimate ground of what is. In other words, the self becomes most fully a self when it thinks its selfhood in relation to God and all that God allows to be. This is the ultimate vantage point, the ultimate exercise in standing back and surveying the entire landscape.

The point can be put in Kantian terms. In Kant's first *Critique*, where he explores the "transcendental ideas"—which are heuristic devices rather than designations for possible objects of experience—the idea of the self stands for the subjective unity of experience; the idea of the world stands for the objective unity of experience; and the idea, or "ideal," of God stands for that which unifies both self and world.[10] Thus, what the self is can be fully understood only in correlation with the notions of world and God.

It is true for both Kant and Rahner that this vital function is played simply by the *idea* of God; while both thinkers hold that God does in fact exist, the actual existence of God is not required for this process of locating the self. Nor is it necessary to have at one's disposal the technical terminology and conceptual inventory of a Kant or a Rahner. Thus, the traditional notion of God as held by the average believer admirably serves this function of constructing the sense of selfhood. To think the idea of God, including God as traditionally understood by Jews and Christians through the ages, is to *place* the self in such a way that the self can most fully become a self. Or, to put the matter in terms borrowed from Søren Kierkegaard, without actually adopting Kierkegaard's philosophy of God and the self, to think the idea of God can bring to awareness the task of becoming a self.[11]

As long as the idea of God, or something similarly ultimate, is kept alive in human culture, this peculiarly human form of self-consciousness is assured.[12] Nor is the atheist excluded. For as long as one grows up in a culture where one inevitably confronts the idea of God, then at least on some level one will also inevitably confront the issue of what it means to be a self, not just in the context of the objects of one's immediate experience, but in the context of the whole of reality.[13] But if the idea of God or the ultimate were to disappear altogether, then, according to Rahner's meditation, we would lose a key dimension of self-consciousness. We would be trapped in a one-dimensional immediacy and would find ourselves in a mere "environment," rather than in a "world," in the fullest sense of that latter term.[14] Or, perhaps more accurately, we would not be able to "find ourselves" at all.

By keeping the notion of God alive in the contemporary context, the enactment model of the divine also keeps alive this vital function that the idea of God has played in numerous cultures through the ages. In fact, the enactment approach to Goddess seems particularly well suited to this task; it is transparent to this function of the God-idea. Enactment theology understands Goddess precisely as a matter of the self being placed in a particular relationship with various dimensions of reality that are other than the self.

Of course, in something like a feminist enactment theology, any essentially Hegelian dialectic of selfhood—the "I" recognizes itself by playing itself off against all that is not "I"—is transmuted, in that the others, in the face of which the self becomes a self, retain their genuine otherness. There can be no suggestion here, in other words, of a subjectivity that negates otherness and ultimately takes it up into a totalitarian unity. And this fact provides a glimpse of the ambivalence of feminist religious consciousness toward postmodernism. On the one hand, feminists, committed as they are to full personhood for women, will be loathe to fully embrace the postmodernists' rejection of the centered self.[15] But, on the other hand, the recognition and even celebration of the otherness of others, and the fact that the self becomes a self only in relation to these others, entails that the self of feminist consciousness will always be "eccentric," i.e., partly outside itself or "de-centered."

Furthermore, there are other, more thoroughly non-Hegelian, ways in which the God-idea can carry on the vital task of constructing the self. For instance, Luce Irigaray, drawing upon the thought of Feuerbach, argues that

> all women, except when they remain submitted to the logic of the essence of man, should imagine a God for themselves, an objective and subjective place or path for the possible assemblage of the self in space and time: a unity of instinct, heart and knowledge. . . . The feeling or experience of a positive, objective and glorious existence for our subjectivity is necessary for us. Such as a God who helps and guides us in our becoming, who holds the measure of our limits— women—and our relation tothe infinite, which inspires our endeavours.[16]

As Elizabeth Grosz points out, Irigaray wishes to posit "not a single, paternal God, whose unity and universality sweeps away a polytheistic pantheon, but sexually specific gods, gods who represent the extension and perfection, the infinite becoming, of sexually specific subjects."[17] Perhaps a radically polysymbolic monotheism, such as a feminist enactment theology, is up to this task.

That the relation that enacts Goddess can energize the task of becoming a self surely makes the Goddess-relation attractive. But why should I suppose that this particular relation is even possible? We take a first step toward establishing its possibility when we note that enactment piety makes it *thinkable and tangible*. To enter a particular relation presupposes that one can, to some extent at least, make clear to oneself the boundaries of that relation; one must be able to pick out these boundaries against the potentially confusing background of the many other kinds of relations in which one might choose to engage.[18] The notion of placing the self in relation to other persons, nature, and the power of being is a complex and abstract idea. Its complexity can be gauged by considering the fact that even to enter into relationship with one other human being entails grappling with a host of details, attitudes, and actions associated with that other. Its abstractness resides in the fact that the relation is supposed to take place not just between the self and a number of individual others, but in some sense also with the many unknown others who make up the human community, and with nature and the power of being. Enactment piety makes the numerous components of this abstract idea graspable by unifying them in the concept of God, and it makes the whole relation tangible by concretizing it in symbols. The word "God" or "Goddess" functions to call to mind the notion of the transcendent source of life and meaning that affects the believer's every thought and action, and this notion can properly be identified with the enacted relation that we have been exploring, or so I have argued. The identification unifies the abstract relation, with its inumerable components, in a concept. Furthermore, natural objects such as rocks and trees, as well as human imaginative constructs, can be employed as symbols which point beyond themselves to the enacted relation that is divinity. In this way the whole relation is made concrete. This is a matter of great practical import, for only a relation that is tangible and ready-to-hand can be actualized.

But this is hardly sufficient to establish the viability of the enacted relation, for even if it successfully addresses the relation's graspability, it leaves the more difficult issue of the relation's existential and moral possibility still in doubt. In order to treat this dimension of the problem, we must carefully qualify enactment piety's claims. First, it can be argued that the enacted relation is not a matter of the individual accomplishing some great moral feat, of treating all beings with compassion and justice, for example, but only of acknowledging the claim of otherness upon one. In other words, to enact the relation that is Goddess is to understand oneself in terms of the responsibilities, as well as the opportunities, one has before other persons, nature, and the power of being. It is to be given a new sense of the meaning of one's being, but not necessarily the power to fulfill all of the duties, both to oneself and to others, that ideally follow from that new way of being. Enacting the relation that is Goddess is, first of all, then, simply a matter of perceiving selfhood and otherness in a new way. It is, once again, a matter of being "placed."

Secondly, it is quite possible that this experience of being placed in an attitude of responsibility before otherness, far from presupposing some great moral self-confidence, will be imbued with a sense of *krisis* (a term used in the Greek New Testament to mean "judgment"): the recognition of responsibility before other persons, nature, and the power of being may be experienced as a form of judgment upon one's way of life.[19] The experience need be no less edifying for that, of course. For the self might here be regarded as having been freed from the confines of its self-destructive illusions about its own being.

Furthermore, even just the recognition of responsibility, the openness to the claim of the otherness of others, is a task that must continually be renewed, rather than something that is accomplished once and for all. Thus, before one can contemplate actually behaving toward the other as one ought to behave, one must acknowledge that just the recognition of how one ought to behave is itself a continual struggle. And it is this recognition that enacts the relation that is Goddess.

But if all of these considerations suggest that the enacted relation is in large measure a matter of how one understands the self, rather than of virtuous behavior on the part of the self, surely we must still demand that at least some virtuous behavior issue from the relation. For the relation would finally be productive of little more than despair if it did nothing but alert us to responsibilities that we could never fulfill. The difficulty facing enactment theology at this point can be highlighted by contrasting it with traditional Jewish and Christian theistic piety. For Jewish belief, human beings are created in the image of God. They have been given not only the ability to see the difference between good and evil, but also the ability to use their freedom to do the good. The image of God in man and woman is the basis for what Leo Baeck has called Judaism's "ethical optimism."[20] But enactment theology is, of course, bereft of this source of optimism.

The Christian tradition has tended to see the matter differently from Judaism. For Christian piety, though human beings have indeed been created in the image of God, the Fall has seriously impaired the moral abilities that would otherwise flow from that origin. Thus, supernatural intervention is required, and it comes in the form of the Christ. The Christ brings with him the grace needed for the believer to do the good. In Augustinian terms, this grace empowers one to live as he or she should. And in the variation worked out in Roman Catholicism via the Council of Trent, human beings can use their freedom to cooperate with divine grace, and through this cooperation, the good can be accomplished. Again, enactment theology apparently comes up empty-handed, for it cannot look to a divine being who provides this kind of empowering grace.

Nor do things look any brighter if we consider the Lutheran model of justifying grace. In that model, grace is not a power which enables the believer to obey God's moral commands, but a divine decree according to which, thanks to the merits of Christ, the sinner is counted as righteous while remaining a sinner. But, of course, enactment theology has no place for a gracious supernatural being who forgives human inabilities to accomplish the good.

But despite all of this, perhaps there is still a place for something akin to grace in enactment piety. It is important to keep in mind that the enacted relation is a relation to otherness. This is a source of difficulty, insofar as it brings with it the responsibilities at issue here, but it may also be a source of strength for the individual attempting to enact the relation that is Goddess. For the various others to whom the individual is now attempting to relate himself or herself are, precisely as other, able to provide resources that the individual does not possess on his or her own. In other words, the task of discharging one's responsibilities to the neighbor, in the widest sense of the term "neighbor," is aided by that very neighbor. The world of nature, for instance, upholds me at the same time that it confronts me with certain responsibilities toward it. And the same can be said for the power of being behind nature, and for the other human beings whom I encounter, especially those other human beings who are part of my own immediate environment. In the end, therefore, there is not only a demand, but also something gracious that confronts me in my attempt to effect a relation with these others. And this allows for at least a modicum of optimism about the possibility of enacting the relation that is Goddess, and successfully discharging one's moral responsibilities in the light of this relation.

There may also be another sense in which the very nature of the relation envisioned by enactment theology makes the realization of that relation more plausible. That is, there may be a way in which the world view associated with enactment piety effectively reinforces the ethical life. In order to see how this is so, we begin with a question: Can there be such a thing as an "ethical world view?" If we return to the work of Emmanuel Levinas for guidance, the answer would apppear to be "no," at least insofar as there is any suggestion of capturing the ethical within a system or totalizing scheme.[21] Once again, Levinas' radical approach to the ethical is by no means obligatory for an enactment theology, but it is consistent with enactment piety and provides fascinating clues about where such a piety might lead. On Levinasian terms, the ethical command cannot be domesticated by translating it into a static set of instructions about human being and the world, and supposing that this exhausts the meaning of the ethical. But however illegitimate this notion of an ethical world view, might it not be legitimate to talk about the "ethical integration of one's world view," meaning that one allows the ethical command to organize the world around itself? In this case there is no suggestion of taking the ethical up into some larger system of meaning that "puts it in its place," which would be impossible, since the ethical demand explodes any attempt to conceptually master or limit it. Rather, the ethical demand itself is what does the organizing or placement.

Enactment piety can be understood in just these terms. When one responds to the demand of the other, she or he is put in a particular relation with nature, other selves, and the power of being. This relation constitutes a new world for the self, which is to say that the ethical imperative represented by the other constitutes the world here.

If it is legitimate to speak of the ethical imperative represented by otherness constituting a world around itself, we must still stay on guard against the illusion that thinking can master the ethical demand. Thus, note that the ethical can create a world only formally, not materially. That is, once again, we would violate the transcendence of the ethical if we attempted to read off it the specific contents of a world view; this would be but another form of the illusory assumption that the moral demand can be cut to the size of our thinking. Instead, what occurs in the enactment of deity is the creation of the formal dimensions of a world view: the self is placed in a position of openness to the otherness of nature, other selves, and the power of being, but there is no suggestion that one can know in advance just what this openness might involve or what content will be received in this relation, nor that one can ever exhaust one's responsibility to the other. This is another example, then, of how enactment piety "places" the self.

Having attempted to guard against any suggestion that the ethical imperative is at the disposal of our thinking, we must now go on to acknowledge that the formal world view created around the ethical does, nonetheless, act back upon its ethical starting point. But it does so only on the level of psychological motivation. One may hold that the good is good in and of itself, and that it does not need anything outside itself to make it worth pursuing. One should behave ethically toward the other simply because that is the right thing to do. But even if the *source* of the "ought" is wholly *sui generis*, it does not follow that the *psychological motivation* for obeying that "ought" cannot be connected with other interests. Indeed, perhaps as many motivating factors as possible should be marshalled on behalf of doing the good, as long as those factors are not in any way themselves immoral. How does this connect with enactment piety? The moral imperative, which is represented by the other, forms the outlines of a world around itself. This formal world view is beholden to the moral imperative, and not vice-versa. But the larger world view has important psychological ramifications for how the self responds to the imperative. For now the ethical imperative is experienced not as a matter of discrete commands, but in terms of a meaningful way of life, indeed of a meaningful cosmos. Thus, while the ethical imperative's validity can never legitimately be reinforced externally, the motivation for obeying it is here surely reinforced by the meaningful world that the imperative brings into being.

Suppose we now step back and survey the landscape we have traversed. We began with a sense of skepticism about whether the relation envisioned by enactment theology is possible. We then investigated the contention that enactment piety does at least make that relation thinkable and tangible, but this left the existential and moral difficulties of effecting the relation untouched. Next, we noted the modesty of what might be regarded as the minimal claims entailed by enactment theology. Much of the enacted relation turns out to be a matter of the self being placed in a new mode of self-understanding vis-à-vis the other, rather than of the self accomplishing heroic moral deeds on behalf of the other. But surely some moral deeds must be possible if enactment piety is to be viable. And enactment piety cannot be as optimistic about the possibility of such deeds as can traditional Judaism and Christianity. Still, we saw that the scenario envisioned by enactment piety is not without an element of grace. And we have noted how the formal world view attached to enactment piety may serve to reinforce ethical behavior.

None of what we have seen demonstrates that the relation that enacts divinity is a real possibility for human beings, nor even that it will prove an attractive challenge to a large number of people. At the same time, our explorations in this chapter should at least lend a degree of plausibility to enactment theology's claims. From this vantage point, the future of the enacted Goddess need not be regarded as entirely bleak.

There is one more attribute of enactment theology that we ought to consider, an attribute that further strengthens its case, but which is different from the ones we have explored up to this point.

Enactment theology, while it may be focused on more purely existential and moral issues, also offers us a particular way in which to conceptualize reality. Of course, enactment theology does not set forth ontological claims akin to those advanced by more traditional theologies; it is not an exercise in metaphysics, at least in the ordinary sense of that term. But we can begin to grasp some of the conceptual possibilities inherent in the enactment approach to theology by considering the relationship between an enactment theology and contemporary natural science. This is an obvious starting point for investigating a theology's conceptual powers, given the hegemony of science in contemporary first-world society when it comes to conceptualizing the world.

The relation between religion and science in the West has often been a troubled one. The two sides have frequently looked upon one another with derision. If feminist religious consciousness is to be our major key to enactment theology, one might initially assume that this hostility will continue even when the sacred has been transformed and Goddess is understood as a relation that we enact. Feminists are, after all, often suspicious of the way in which science attempts to manipulate nature, forcing her to give up her secrets, rather than appreciating it as a dimension of the holy. For someone such as Rosemary Radford Ruether, for instance, the scientific method brings to mind Francis Bacon and his use of images of rape and torture to describe how science investigates the natural world.[22]

But there is a different way of reading the scientific enterprise, and a way of seeing enactment theology as particularly supportive of scientific exploration of the world. Consider three things: First, enactment piety involves a sense of connection with nature and the universe that makes the exploration of the natural world especially attractive. Second, enactment theology brings with it no ontological assumptions that could interfere with the legitimate exercise of the scientific method. There is nothing in the enactment world view that dictates, for instance, that the universe must have begun in some particular fashion or that causality must be understood in some special way. Third, while enactment theology brings no ontological dogmatism or New Age metaphysical chicanery to bear, it does bring with it the aforementioned ethical dimension. Thus, the enactment perspective does nothing to thwart the scientific enterprise as such, but may offer insights into the use of science and its effects. As a matter of fact, the ethical dimension of enactment piety is strikingly consistent with a particular way of reading the scientific method. Rather than thinking of that method in terms of the Baconian rack, one can see it as a profoundly relational undertaking, not only in that the desire to understand the natural world can flow from one's sense of participation in nature, but also inasmuch as science involves constantly giving one's thinking over to others. Science is a communal affair, in that one's own claims can never be accepted until one's experimental results have been reproduced by others. Adherence to the scientific method is, in this sense, an exercise in cognitive self-transcendence: what I seem to know about the world on the basis of my own thinking cannot be accepted as valid, even by myself, until the limitations of my single perspective have been canceled out by having my work taken up by others.

One who embraces enactment theology need not endorse any particular application of scientific knowledge, of course, nor must she or he be enamored of the technologizing of our society. But enactment theology does provide a unique vantage point from which to appreciate the beauty of scientific inquiry. Clearly, enactment theology can result in a much more productive relationship with science than is possible for traditional theism. While the traditional theistic world view can be made compatible with modern and contemporary science, such compatibility is often a function of putting science and theology on completely separate tracks so that they cannot interfere with one another. This is especially evident when one recalls how traditional theism is now privatized.

But enactment theology's potentially productive juxtaposition with natural science is not its only strength of a philosophical, conceptual sort. For enactment theology gives us, after all, a way not just of symbolizing the ultimate, but of thinking about it. Suppose that, consistent with at least some currents of the age, one is skeptical about any remotely metaphysical perspective, whether it be the traditional metaphysics of a Plato or Aquinas, or the oracular pronouncements of the later Heidegger. Any such metaphysical explorations, says the

skeptic, deal with matters about which we simply cannot know anything. Enactment theology allows us to speak meaningfully about the
ultimate even in the midst of this skepticism. For, on the one hand,
the enactment perspective has to do not with some mysterious supernatural reality, but with a choice that we ourselves might make about
how we shall relate to what is. But, on the other hand, this enacted
relation is surely a candidate for ultimacy. It is a relation that encompasses the self, other persons, nature, and the undergirding power of
nature in a unified whole. Thinking about the enacted relation is a
way of thinking about the whole of things.

This ability to conceptualize the whole of things fits with Clifford
Geertz's claim that a religion provides its adherents with "conceptions
of a general order of existence."[23] Yet this particular conception of a
general order of existence, despite the fact that it encompasses everything in a unified whole, is not the kind of tyrannical totalizing scheme
that is the familiar *bête noire* of postmodern theory. This is so for two
reasons. First, as we noted in our discussion of how the ethical can constitute a world, the whole at issue here is a function precisely of relation
with otherness. Thus the unity that appears is not a matter of some set
of ideas that allegedly categorizes and conceptually masters everything
that exists, thereby reducing the other to the same. Rather, it is a matter of being placed in a relation to all else that exists, in an attitude of
openness and responsibility. There can be no suggestion of conceptual
control here, for openness toward otherness means being at the disposal of the other. Second, the concept of the whole that issues from
enactment theology is not a "metanarrative" in the most literal sense of
the term, i.e., a perspective that one claims is beyond narrative in that it
describes something that is objectively given, something that simply
impresses itself upon our cognitive equipment rather than flowing from
our narrative powers. On the contrary, this whole is a relation that is
entirely optional, perhaps even unlikely, and it recognizes itself as such.
Thus, it recognizes itself as a narrative, as one way to tell the story of
our relation to the world, to fit things together in a coherent fashion.

At the same time, none of this entails that enactment theology sees itself as merely fiction. For one thing, though there are no traditional metaphysical claims included in the enactment model,

ontological claims of another sort are clearly involved. Much is pre-supposed here about the character of human being, the world of nature, and the power of being. More important, the enacted relation itself, which enactment theology equates with deity, is held to be eminently real. Relations do not have the same ontological status as physical entities, for example, but they are no less real. In short, to say that God is an optional relation, a way that persons may choose to relate to other persons, nature, and the power of being, is nothing like saying that enactment piety is a form of "fictive religiosity."[24] This is not a theology of "as if."[25]

Any attempt to evaluate the potential validity of enactment theology's reality claims must recognize that the enacted Goddess-relation is not a projection, at least not in the philosophically pejorative sense of the term. Opponents of theism such as Feuerbach and Freud charge that God is not real, but simply something that human beings project onto the cosmos. But enactment theology does not entail any belief in occult entities or supernatural beings. The only kind of projection that it involves is one that is part of the very structure of human being: one projects various possibilities into the future, in order to act upon them. Such possibilities, if they are genuine, can be *realized*; they are not exercises in self-deception. The notion of relating to other persons, nature, and the power of being in such as way as to enact Goddess is not the projection of an imaginary entity, but rather the projection of a possibility to be realized.

One of the attractive features of traditional piety was that it provided the basis for a fruitful way of thinking about the world. In other words, the intellectual dimension of piety connects with the existential dimension at this point. We want to be able to understand the world. Thus, any approach to the world that does not engage the intellect will remain, at best, unsatisfying. And the moral dimension may also link up with the intellectual dimension here, inasmuch as any piety that neglects the attempt to understand the world will be not just unsatisfying, but also irresponsible. Enactment theology's potential ability to satisfy the cognitive, intellectual demands placed upon religion is another indication, then, that the enacted Goddess may have a place in future piety.[26]

The Western notion of God is in desperate need of transformation. Traditional theism's concept of God as a supernatural personal agent is unavoidably privatized when it comes up against the peculiarly contemporary version of the problem of theodicy. The enacted Goddess who appears in our reading of feminist theology embodies the requisite transformation. She is, paradoxically, the full-fledged divinity who has animated Western religious consciousness through the centuries. Her devotees need not huddle within the confines of the private sphere: she calls them forth into the worlds of nature and history; she graces her followers with the kind of powerful religious experience that flows only from a deity who is both immanent and transcendent; and she evokes a spirit of worship and devotion that would not be unfamiliar to religious persons of the past.

While there may be other transformations of God, it should not be surprising that one potent instance arises from feminist religious consciousness. Any transformation possessing the existential force to engender healthy ultimate concern must spring from genuine human struggle. The rise of feminist consciousness is one of the most important examples of such struggle in the modern West. Contrary to the defensive protestations of the political right, this consciousness, and feminist *religious* consciousness in particular, is almost invariably an expansive and affirmative vision. It is fertile soil for the rebirth of divinity.

Epilogue

Theodicy Revisited

*I*t will be useful, by way of conclusion to our study, to return briefly to the problem of theodicy. It was theodicy, after all, in its peculiarly contemporary guise, that undid the God of traditional theism and forced the transformation of God. A consideration of how theodicy impinges upon enactment piety will afford us a final evaluative glimpse at the enacted deity.

The easy answer to the question about how theodicy relates to enactment theology is, of course, to say that an enactment theology simply escapes the problem of theodicy altogether, since it does not assert the existence of a personal God who could be regarded as responsible for evil. But a critic might not want to let enactment theology off so easily. Suppose that he or she were to say that the problem of evil does plague enactment theology, but that it simply takes a different form. By naively celebrating human potential and holding that human beings can enact just and creative relations with the other, enactment theology has, so its critics might argue, traded the problem of theodicy for the problem of anthropodicy: How can one justify such confidence in human abilities in the face of the horrible evils that human beings visit upon one another? Doesn't an enactment theology have just as big a problem in the face of the Nazi Holocaust, for instance, as traditional theism does? Indeed, might it not have a bigger problem?

The first defensive maneuver to be undertaken here is to recall that enactment theology need not make naive claims about human moral ability. Rather, as we have seen, the heart of enactment theology is the conviction that a self can be placed in a relationship wherein she or he understands herself or himself as responsible to the other. Enactment theology is not fatally undermined by the observation that the discharge of that responsibility does not follow automatically upon its recognition. And even if we cannot always count on human beings to act upon their highest convictions, certainly it is best to at least begin with the sort of convictions that encourage sensitivity toward the other. Feminist theology's emphasis on overcoming destructive relations with other persons and with nature is, in other words, surely a laudable starting point. Indeed, there is a kind of ethical energy about much feminist piety that is a necessary antidote to what has been called, with striking aptness, the "moral exhaustion" of contemporary American society in the face of problems such as the creation of a permanent underclass in this country.[1] In addition, it is essential to keep in mind Sharon Welch's warning that we must avoid the despair that results from falsely assuming that the only worthwhile moral effort is one that results in a total solution to the ills it addresses. That assumption is based on a desire for omnipotence and control; Welch points us instead toward an "ethic of risk."[2]

But it should also be reiterated that enactment piety is not simply a function of the human. The feminist theology that we have been taking as paradigmatic of the enactment approach also emphasizes the role of nature and the power of being, and these are essential elements of the enacted relation. What that relation is supposed to accomplish is, at least in part, a result of the self being sustained and empowered by its participation in nature and the force that animates it. In this instance, it is by no means entirely true to say that theology is simply anthropology.[3]

All of these considerations have to do, however, with moral or human evil. What about so-called natural evil? The suffering imposed upon human beings and other animals by their own natural environment has also traditionally been an important part of the problem of theodicy. Two considerations, in particular, indicate the difference between enactment theology and more traditional theological approaches to the problem of natural evil. First, enactment theology, especially in its feminist guise, may wish to reevaluate what counts as natural evil. It is reasonable to expect a thinker such as Carol Christ, for example, to suggest that one ought not to focus narrowly upon human interests and needs. What appears as an instance of natural evil from a limited human perspective may be a perfectly healthy phenomenon from the vantage point of the larger natural world.

Second, an enactment theology can confront natural evil without the paralyzing resentment against God that is sometimes at least an unconscious element in more traditional piety. For the devotee of the enacted Goddess, as opposed to the follower of the personal God of traditional theism, there is no agonizing "Why?" The natural world is understood as operating according to its own immanent principles. There is no one at which to shake one's fist, for the suffering visited upon us by nature is not a function of any conscious, responsible force. As a result, one can get on with the practical task of attempting to alleviate the suffering that nature causes, rather than feeling the need to explain how it can happen.

As a general evaluation of enactment theology's response to evil, we can say that, over against both moral and natural evil, enactment theology can accomplish what any theodicy must accomplish if it is to be successful: it can locate evil below the level of the ultimate. The reality of evil cannot be denied. It is little more than a mental game or a psychological subterfuge, for example, to argue that evil is a privation of the good, and therefore has no substance. Whatever the metaphysics of evil may be, its effects upon human life are real enough. Thus, the goal of a theodicy ought to be not to deny the existence of evil, but to show that evil neither infects nor derives from the ultimate dimension of reality; evil is real, but there is something higher than evil, something that provides a vantage point beyond it and resources for combating it. And this is something that an enactment theology can surely do. For the enactment model looks to a relation that corrects the disrelations, what Ruether calls the "dualisms," that are the source of our inhumanity to one another. It sees something beyond the destructive mindset of man versus woman and power versus powerlessness.[4] And it sees something above natural evil, in that the relation it seeks to enact allows one to understand that not everything that appears evil from the human vantage point is in fact evil. In addition, it seeks a relation that will put one in a position to help negate the suffering that nature sometimes does visit upon the other.

All of this leads, finally, to a consideration of the one sense in which all theology is, indeed must be, a form of anthropology (or perhaps of Mary Daly's gyn/ecology). Let us suppose, for a moment, that traditional theism is still viable and that the God of traditional theism exists. While the philosopher may be interested in God in and of Godself, the religious person, and by extension the theologian, is always concerned with God in relation to us. Religion is a thoroughly practical affair. Thus, even if the God of theism is perfectly real, our theological response to him must always be a form of anthropology, in the sense that we must be concerned with what the existence and nature of God mean for human life and behavior. Elie Wiesel has remarked on how odd it seems, at least initially, that when God revealed himself at Sinai, he told us nothing at all about his own inner being. Shouldn't one expect some kind of glimpse into the divine essence from such a revelation? What else can revelation mean? What God did reveal at Sinai, of course, according to Jewish piety, was what he expects of his people, not any secrets about the divine nature.[5] Traditional Jewish theology, with its focus upon the Torah, and traditional Christian theology, with its emphasis on the God who reveals himself in the incarnate redeemer, are both anthropological in this important, and wholly orthodox, sense.

It is a reliable dictum, then—one need not go so far as to call it a definition—that religion is concerned with what it means to be a human being in the face of the ultimate, however the ultimate be conceived. Feminist enactment theology is no exception to this rule; it is, in fact, a powerful exemplification of the dictum. The feminist theologies that have been of concern to us here not only attempt to understand what it means to be a human being within the context of the larger universe of being, they try to provide resources for the practical realization of that meaning. They push us to achieve a sensitive and creative relation to the fullness of being around us. And by so doing, they accomplish the very essence of the theological task.

.

Notes

Introduction

1. Alistair Kee, *The Way of Transcendence: Christian Faith without Belief in God* (Harmondsworth: Penguin, 1971), ix.
2. Gordon D. Kaufman, *In Face of Mystery: A Constructive Theology* (Cambridge, Mass: Harvard, 1993), 4.

I. Has Religion Been Reborn?

1. "Religion within the limits of reason alone" is, of course, Immanuel Kant's phrase. See *Religion within the Limits of Reason Alone*, trans. Theodore M. Greene and Hoyt H. Hudson (New York: Harper and Row, 1960). Also see Thomas Jefferson, *The Jefferson Bible: the Life and Morals of Jesus of Nazareth* (Boston: Beacon, 1989).
2. The influential notion of a "religionless Christianity" arises in the context of Dietrich Bonhoeffer's prison meditations on the nature of Christian faith in the contemporary world. See his *Letters and Papers from Prison*, enlarged edition, ed. Eberhard Bethge, trans. Reginald H. Fuller et al. (New York: Macmillan, 1971). The representatives of the

so-called death of God theology who came closest to recommending the Jeffersonian Jesus were probably William Hamilton and Paul Van Buren. See William Hamilton, *The New Essence of Christianity* (New York: Association Press, 1961), and Paul M. Van Buren, *The Secular Meaning of the Gospel* (New York: Macmillan, 1963).

3. For example, George Gallup, Jr. and Jim Castelli, *The People's Religion: American Faith in the 90's* (New York: Macmillan, 1989), and Kenneth L. Woodward, "Heaven," *Newsweek*, March 27, 1989, 52–55.

4. Engaging arguments about the role of religion in American public life and the prejudices against it in some quarters of American society are provided by Stephen Carter, *The Culture of Disbelief: How American Law and Politics Trivialize Religious Devotion* (New York: Basic Books, 1993); and Garry Wills, *Under God: Religion and American Politics* (New York: Simon and Schuster, 1990). Wills's book is full of the kind of fascinating insights and contentions that one finds in most of his work. In this book, however, he is too uncritical of the polling information on American religiosity. Compare my remarks below on the polling data.

5. *The Chronicle of Higher Education* 38/30 (April 1, 1992): A6.

6. Ibid., A3.

7. See Peter Steinfels, "Psychiatrists' Manual Shifts Stance on Religious and Spiritual Problems," *New York Times*, 10 February, 1994, A16.

8. The term "postmodern," or "postmodernity," suggests simply the period that follows modernity, whereas the term "postmodernism" is usually taken to refer to a self-conscious movement that espouses certain positions that are in opposition to modernity. See, for example, the introductory remarks by Joseph Natoli and Linda Hutcheon in *A Postmodern Reader*, ed. Joseph Natoli and Linda Hutcheon (New York: State University of New York Press, 1993), vii–xiv.

9. For an analysis of the religious components of the conflict, see Michael Sells, "Bosnia: Some Religious Dimensions of Genocide," *Religious Studies News* 9/2 (May 1994): 4–5. The Russians were reportedly hesitant to join in the international condemnation of the Serbs, not only because of their ethnic ties with the Serbs, but also because the Serbs are fellow Orthodox Christians.

10. See Jean-François Lyotard, *The Postmodern Condition: A Report on Knowledge*, trans. Geoff Bennington and Brian Massumi (Minneapolis: University of Minnesota, 1984), xxiv.

11. At the same time, it should be noted that one faces a version of the chicken and the egg dilemma here: do religious conservatives take politically and socially conservative positions because they are religiously conservative, or do they embrace religious conservatism because they are socially and politically conservative? A parallel question holds for those who are religiously as well as socially and politically liberal. This is an important question, inasmuch as an answer to it would go a long way in revealing whether religion is genuinely formative of American life, or more often merely an epiphenomenon.

12. Stephen Hawking, *A Brief History of Time: From the Big Bang to Black Holes* (New York: Bantam, 1988). Note Carl Sagan's introductory comments on page x, according to which, "This is also a book about God . . . or perhaps about the absence of God."

13. Some of the most impressive work on the relation of religion and science continues to be done by Ian Barbour. See, for example, *Religion in An Age of Science*, vol. 1 of the Gifford Lectures 1989–91, (San Francisco: Harper and Row, 1990).

14. Harold Bloom, *The American Religion: the Emergence of the Post-Christian Nation* (New York: Simon and Schuster, 1992).

15. Robert N. Bellah, Richard Madsen, William M. Sullivan, Ann Swidler, and Steven M. Tipton, *Habits of the Heart: Individualism and Commitment in American Life* (Berkeley: University of California, 1985), 221.

16. The study was led by C. Kirk Hadaway of the United Church of Christ. The finding is reported in Kenneth L. Woodward, "The Rites of Americans," *Newsweek*, November 29, 1993, 80.

17. Robert Wuthnow, "The Future of Mainline Protestantism." Presented as one of the Frances Youngker Vosburgh Lectures at Drew Theological School, October 1993. Reprinted in *The Drew Connection* (Winter 1994): 8.

18. For example, *Christianity and the Encounter of the World Religions* (New York: Columbia University, 1963), 4. The University of Chicago historian of religions, Jonathan Z. Smith, in his evaluation of the academic study of religion, especially as carried out within the American Academy of Religion, observes that "Tillich remains the unacknowledged theoretician of our entire enterprise." "Connections," *Journal of the American Academy of Religion* 58 (Spring 1990):6.

19. It should be noted, however, that when Tillich's definition is put in the context of his whole theological system, normative considerations come into play. Given that "our ultimate concern is that which determines our being or non-being," the only legitimate object of ultimate concern is being-itself. See Paul Tillich, *Systematic Theology*, 3 vols. (Chicago: University of Chicago Press, 1951–63), 1: 14.

20. See Thomas Luckmann, *The Invisible Religion: the Problem of Religion in Modern Society* (New York:Macmillan, 1970).

21. Clifford Geertz, "Religion as a Cultural System," in *The Interpretation of Cultures* (New York: Basic Books, 1973), 90.

22. Luckmann, 42.

23. Hence, Carol Christ's feminist religious thought is "thealogy," from the Greek *thea*, Goddess. Thealogy is a term that Christ attributes to Naomi Goldenberg. See Carol P. Christ, *Laughter of Aphrodite: Reflections on a Journey to the Goddess* (San Francisco: Harper and Row, 1987), xvii, n.1.

24. The family resemblance theory is derived from paragraph #67 of Ludwig Wittgenstein's *Philosophical Investigations*, 3d ed., trans. G. E. M. Anscombe (New York: Macmillan, 1968).

25. The attempt to define "religion" and the attempt to define "God" are, however, not necessarily the same in *all* respects. The referent of "religion" is not some discrete entity. Thus, the phenomenon of religion is itself, in part, a mental construct. The referent of "God," on the other hand, has traditionally been understood as a self-identical being, the Supreme Being. If such a being exists, it is no human mental construct; it is not unified by our interpretive decisions. But even if we were to assume this traditional position on the being of God, reflection about

God over the ages has resulted in so many different views of the specific attributes of God and of God's relation to the world, that interpretive judgments would clearly be required in order to choose among them.

26. We shall discover below, however, that feminist religious consciousness makes the distinction between monotheism and polytheism more complex than it once seemed.

27. For an important contemporary example, see Robert P. Scharlemann, *The Being of God: Theology and the Experience of Truth* (New York: Seabury, 1981).

28. Friedrich Schleiermacher, *The Christian Faith*, ed. H. R. Mackintosh and J. S. Stewart (Philadelphia: Fortress, 1976), 16.

29. Ibid.

30. See Paul Tillich, *Systematic Theology* 1; Karl Rahner, *Foundations of Christian Faith: An Introduction to the Idea of Christianity*, trans. William V. Dych (New York: Seabury, 1978).

31. See, especially, Hermann Cohen, *Religion of Reason out of the Sources of Judaism*, trans. Simon Kaplan (New York: Frederick Ungar, 1972).

32. The most important exception here is probably the work of Rudolph Bultmann, whose project of demythologizing the Christian message, including traditional Christian God-talk, is spurred by a sense that the modern scientific world view renders much of the intellectual framework of the Bible problematic for contemporary readers. See, for example, Rudolph Bultmann, "New Testament and Mythology," in *Kerygma and Myth*, ed. Hans Werner Bartsch, revised trans. Reginald H. Fuller (New York: Harper and Row, 1961), 1–44.

33. Of course this need not imply that the transformations worked out by the great modern theologians are irrelevant to what is at issue here. On the contrary, while those transformations originally may have been a function of purely intraphilosophical forces, they can usefully be relocated and reinterpreted by graphing them on the axis of social and religious change.

34. Now that I have championed a substantive definition of religion and an analysis of continuity and change that draws upon it, it is possible, and

also necessary, to make some technical clarifications. We can begin by returning to the Wittgensteinian notion of family resemblance concepts. According to the family resemblance theory, not all uses of the word "religion" need to point to the very same characteristics. I may call "A," "B," "C," and "D" each "religious." Suppose that phenomenon "A" has the following characteristics: it is a ritual, it has an ethical dimension, and it has to do with the supernatural. Phenomenon "B" has an ethical dimension, has to do with the supernatural, and involves attention to an authoritative text. Phenomenon "C" has to do with the supernatural, involves attention to an authoritative text, and includes a concern with immortality. Phenomenon "D" involves attention to an authoritative text, includes a concern for immortality, and emphasizes extraordinary experiential states. Each of these is an instance of religion in a way analogous to how each of the Smith children can be said to "look like a Smith": it is not a matter of the same characteristics in each case, but of overlapping characteristics. Phenomenon "D" has no specific characteristics in common with Phenomenon "A," just as the youngest Smith child may look nothing like the oldest, yet "A" and "D" are both recognizable as instances of religion, just as the oldest and the youngest child are both recognizable as Smiths, inasmuch as each does resemble *other* members of the family.

How may this family resemblance theory be applied more exactly to the approach I am taking in this book? "Religion" can be acknowledged to be a family resemblance concept. But things get a bit more complicated when we turn to particular religious traditions. On the one hand, terms such as "Judaism" and "Christianity" may themselves suggest family resemblance concepts: not all of the instances to which we apply the term "Christianity" share the very same characteristics. On the other hand, it is surely conceivable that, amid the flux of overlapping characteristics, there may be one or two characteristics that do attach to almost all uses of a term such as "Christianity" or "Judaism" (especially considering that these traditions, or at least certain subdivisions of them, have definite institutional boundaries). My contention is that "God" is just such a constant characteristic where American Judaism and Christianity (and most of the religious movements that they influence) are concerned.

Now the notion of God, in turn, may be a family resemblance concept, as I mention above. My definition of God as "the transcendent source of life and meaning that ultimately informs the believer's every thought and action" overlaps with how the notion of God has been used down through the centuries in the Jewish and Christian traditions. To the extent that I pick out only this one formulation, my definition might be said to be stipulative. But because of its family resemblance with the whole tradition of God-talk in Judaism and Christianity, it is not stipulative in the sense of being purely arbitrary. Furthermore, it seems to me that, as with terms such as "Judaism" and "Christianity," it may well be that there are in fact at least some characteristics that are nearly constant in the history of Jewish and Christian God-talk (see pp. 42–43 above on what it would be like to imagine Jewish or Christian God-talk without the characteristics contained in my definition). Thus, while I am willing to entertain the family resemblance approach up to a point, I am also willing to think in terms of some essential core of Jewish and Christian God-talk, at the very least in a stipulative sense, if not also in a realist one.

All of this puts us in a better position to grasp how continuity and change play themselves out here. I have looked for both the continuity and the change within talk about God, i.e., within the *content* of Jewish and Christian religiosity. More specifically, I have suggested that my definition of God can be read as an essential core that remains intact amidst different formulations of God, indeed that this core can only be preserved through talk about God that is different from some of the formulations that expressed it in the past. One way to see what remains relatively continuous here in the midst of change is to note that, while we are operating in the realm of the content of religion—we have zeroed in on particular beliefs as definitive of religion rather than some function of religion—we can nonetheless analyze this content in such a way as to find a functional sub-dimension. For while a "transcendent source of life" perhaps suggests a more straightforwardly substantive approach, a "source of meaning that ultimately informs the believer's every thought and action" is functional. This functional sub-dimension of my definition of God strengthens its claim to stand out as what is constant in the midst of change or difference. That is, in addition to the fact that this particular content *should* be held constant in the midst of changes in other contents of piety (again, recall the argument on pp. 42–43 above), its functional dimension perhaps makes it more durable than those aspects of God-talk that are purely matters of belief and not at all of function, (e.g., the notion of God as a personal being, or the notion of God as impersonal). Particular beliefs are often fairly easily undermined by shifts in culture and experience, while human functional demands seem harder to alter.

But to pick out this particular content—"the transcendent source of life and meaning that ultimately informs the believer's every thought and action"—and hold it constant *relative to change in other contents of God-talk* is not to suppose that it is constant or unchanging *relative to itself.* Jacques Derrida's perspective is instructive here: this particular content is not some perfectly self-identical content of consciousness, some pure presence. Rather, it is itself a text. Thus it is what it is only through the "detour of the sign," and, as a result, is always different from itself (Jacques Derrida, *Margins of Philosophy*, trans. Alan Bass [Chicago: University of Chicago, 1982], 9). And, in reality, this particular content can never be held entirely constant even relative to other contents, given that it will always be affected to some degree by the other contents with which it is connected.

II. The Subtle Demise of Traditional Theism

1. Of course, the fact that this was indeed a transformation can perhaps only be grasped from the vantage point afforded by modern historical consciousness. Note that such a transformation is by no means necessarily a matter of corruption or devolution, a fact that Roman Catholic reflection on the development of doctrine has been at pains to point out since the nineteenth century. For a contemporary example of such reflection, see Bernard Lonergan, *The Way to Nicea: The Dialectical Development of Trinitarian Theology*, trans. Conn O'Donovan (Philadelphia: Westminster, 1976).

2. It is possible, of course, that if Americans' notions of God were plumbed to a greater depth than most polls are able to do, we would

discover that those notions are often farther from traditional theism than we might originally have imagined. One tantalizing suggestion of this is provided by the response of American Roman Catholics to a survey that asked them to pick a statement about God's relation to the world with which they agreed. Only 18 percent chose "God transcends the world but is actively involved in the world," which surely expresses traditional Christian theism. A full 39 percent opted for "The world is part of God, but God is greater and larger than the world," which can best be described as an expression of panentheism. 15 percent chose "God and the world are one," which suggests pantheism. 24 percent agreed with the statement that "Human beings are part of God." Only 3 percent chose "God sets the world in motion but does not play an active role in the world," with its Deistic cast, and only 1 percent agreed with the statement that "God transcends the world, entering the world infrequently." See Jim Castelli and Joseph Gremillion, *The Emerging Parish: The Notre Dame Study of Catholic Life Since Vatican II* (San Francisco: Harper and Row, 1987), 154.

3. The situation for Judaism in the same period was more complicated. On the one hand, the Jews were under the thumb of the Roman Empire. On the other hand, there remained in the land of Israel a fully formed Jewish religious and social establishment that was recognized by the Romans and that was allowed to exercise a degree of control over daily events in Israel, at least until the destruction of the Temple in 70 C.E.

4. See Peter Berger, *The Sacred Canopy: Elements of a Sociological Theory of Religion* (Garden City, N.Y.: Doubleday-Anchor, 1967), and Robert N. Bellah, "The Triumph of Secularism," *Religion and Intellectual Life* 1 (Winter 1984): 13–26.

5. According to *The American Heritage Dictionary* (1st ed., ed. William Morris [Boston: Houghton Mifflin, 1971], 1334), the word "theodicy" derives from the Greek *theos*, "God," and *dikē*, "judgment." It entails judging God's justice and goodness. More specifically, theodicy is the attempt to defend that justice and goodness in the face of evil and suffering.

6. Note Geertz's analysis of the religious significance of the several forms of cognitive chaos. See "Religion as a Cultural System," 99–108.

7. This is, in Bernhard Anderson's words, "the Deuteronomic formula for success and failure: obedience to Yahweh's commands will be rewarded with victory and prosperity; disobedience will bring the divine judgment of suffering and failure. This rather neat doctrine of reward and punishment, which may have arisen out of ceremonies of covenant renewal when the formulas of divine blessings and curses were solemnly recited, runs through the whole Deuteronomic History." Bernhard W. Anderson, *Understanding the Old Testament*, 3d ed. (Englewood Cliffs, N.J.: Prentice-Hall, 1975), 111.

8. E.E. Evans-Pritchard, *Witchcraft, Oracles and Magic Among the Azande* (Oxford: Oxford University Press, 1937).

9. Evans-Pritchard is at pains to point out, though, that the Azande are as aware as we are of the proximate causes of these events within what we would call the natural order. See 67ff.

10. Ibid., 63–4.

11. Ibid., 72.

12. Note, however, that both the theistic response and the Azande response provide some measure of control and thus help avoid chaos. The theistic approach does so by offering an ultimately reassuring explanation of evil and suffering, the Azande by providing a social response to the acts of witchcraft that cause the suffering.

13. For a philosophically astute analysis of this phenomenon, see Edith Wyschogrod, *Spirit in Ashes: Hegel, Heidegger, and Man-Made Mass Death* (New Haven: Yale, 1985). Wyschogrod is more concerned with the effect of the "death event" upon our notion of self, however, than upon our notion of God.

14. The most significant genre of modern theology here is undoubtedly constituted by Jewish responses to the Holocaust. Two quite different responses, both important, are Richard Rubenstein, *After Auschwitz: Radical Theology and Contemporary Judaism* (Indianapolis: Bobbs-Merrill, 1966), and Emil L. Fackenheim, *To Mend the World: Foundations of Future Jewish Thought* (New York: Schocken, 1982).

15. *King Lear*, IV.i.36.

16. I am using "nature" and "natural world" here in their now rather old-fashioned sense as referring to a realm distinguishable from human beings and their history.

17. See, for instance, Hans-Georg Gadamer, *Truth and Method*, trans. ed. Garrett Barden and John Cumming (New York: Continuum, 1975), and Richard Palmer, *Hermeneutics: Interpretation Theory in Schleiermacher, Dilthey, Heidegger, and Gadamer* (Evanston: Northwestern, 1969).

18. The relation between objective and subjective conceptual privatization is such that the first may certainly lead to the second: one reflects upon the dynamics of meaning taking place objectively and makes them part of one's own consciousness. But it is also possible for one to embrace an idiosyncratic kind of subjective conceptual privatization, i.e., one without any objective foundation in the larger context of meaning in which one finds oneself; one thinks of God as irrelevant to certain spheres, even though there are no larger processes forcing one to do so. Note also that objective conceptual privatization might, in its own way, be deemed a structural phenomenon, but that it still makes sense to distinguish objective conceptual privatization, along with subjective conceptual privatization, from what I am calling structural privatization. Conceptual privatization, of both the subjective and objective varieties, is primarily a function of meaning, while structural privatization is primarily a function of material forces and of power. Of course, as was noted earlier, structural privatization may at some points impinge upon the realm of meaning and effect conceptual privatization.

19. It follows that transcendence and immanence cannot be opposed in the way that some schools of Christian thought, especially neo-orthodox theology, sometimes suggest that they can. On this matter, see Kathryn Tanner, *God and Creation in Christian Theology: Tyranny or Empowerment?* (Oxford: Basil Blackwell, 1988). The fact that transcendence and immanence are not antithetical but, rather, complementary, will be important for understanding the element of transcendence in feminist theology. See Chapter III herein.

20. See Karen Armstrong, *A History of God: The 4000-Year Quest of Judaism, Christianity, and Islam* (New York: Alfred A. Knopf, 1993), 83–86.

21. Psalm 46:1, in the *New Revised Standard Version*, National Council of Churches of Christ in the United States of America, 1989.

22. This is nowhere more impressively argued than in Ernest Becker, *The Denial of Death* (New York: Free Press, 1973).

23. See "Gilgamesh in Search of Immortality," in *Essential Sacred Writings from Around the World*, ed. Mircea Eliade (San Francisco: Harper Collins, 1967), 325–34.

24. Quoted in Mitchell Stephens, "Jacques Derrida Experiences the Impossible," *New York Times Magazine*, January 23, 1994, 25.

25. Bloom, *The American Religion*, 29.

III. Continuity in Change: God Transformed

1. Schleiermacher's God, while not literally a personal supreme being, is still perceived, from the vantage point of the feeling of absolute dependence, as love. Indeed, the assertion that "God is love" is the single most important description of God for Schleiermacher. See *The Christian Faith*, 727–32. And see Richard R. Niebuhr, "Schleiermacher and the Names of God," in *Schleiermacher as Contemporary, Journal for Theology and the Church*, vol. 7, ed. Robert W. Funk (New York: Herder and Herder, 1970), 176–205. In a similar fashion, Tillich's God is no supernatural being, but one may still use personal imagery to speak of this God in some instances, in that God, as being-itself, is the ground of personhood. See *Systematic Theology* 1:244–5. Cf. Sallie McFague, who steers clear of the notion of God as a supernatural person apart from the world, but holds that personal metaphors are indispensable for speaking about God. See her *Models of God: Theology for an Ecological, Nuclear Age* (Philadelphia: Fortress, 1987), 18–19.

2. This turn to the subject is one of the constitutive elements of what has been termed "Protestant liberalism," a loosely allied school of thought that includes figures such as Albrecht Ritschl, Wilhelm Hermann, and Adolf von Harnack. While twentieth-century Protestant theologians such as Bultmann and Tillich imbibe some of the neo-orthodox protest against this liberal theology, they nonetheless retain the turn to the subject from Schleiermacher's method. And there is a powerful current

in modern Catholic thought that also follows the turn to the subject. Important names in this group include Maurice Blondel, Joseph Marechal, Karl Rahner, and Bernard Lonergan.

3. Elsewhere I have argued that Tillich's whole system can be grasped via the experience of empowerment. See my *Symbol and Empowerment: Paul Tillich's Post-Theistic System* (Macon, Ga.: Mercer, 1985).

4. See Part IV of the system, "Life and the Spirit," in *Systematic Theology* 3:9–294.

5. The phrase is originally Hegel's, but Mark C. Taylor adopts and adapts it to describe the all-encompassing matrix of language. See *Erring: A Postmodern A/Theology* (Chicago: University of Chicago, 1984), 112.

6. See, for example, *Systematic Theology* 1:156; 216.

7. See, for instance, Delwin Brown, Ralph E. James, Jr., and Gene Reeves, eds., *Process Philosophy and Christian Thought* (Indianapolis: Bobbs-Merill, 1971); John B. Cobb and David Ray Griffin, *Process Theology: An Introductory Exposition* (Philadelphia: Westminster, 1976); John B. Cobb, *A Christian Natural Theology Based on the Thought of Alfred North Whitehead* (Philadelphia: Westminster, 1965).

8. The quotation is from Alfred North Whitehead, *Process and Reality: An Essay in Cosmology* (New York: Harper and Row, 1960), 532. For process theodicies, see David Ray Griffin, *God, Power, and Evil: A Process Theodicy* (Philadelphia: Westminster, 1976); and Hans Jonas, "The Concept of God After Auschwitz: A Jewish Voice," *The Journal of Religion* 67 (January 1987):1–13.

9. See, for example, Lewis S. Ford, "Divine Persuasion and the Triumph of Good," in *Process Philosophy and Christian Thought*, 287–304. The idea that even entities without minds can be lured by God is a function of Whitehead's "reformed subjectivist principle." See *Process and Reality*, 252.

10. John Macquarrie, *In Search of Deity: An Essay in Dialectical Theism* (New York: Crossroad, 1987), 180.

11. His classic work is *A Theology of Liberation: History, Politics and Salvation*, trans. and ed. Sr. Caridad Inda and John Eagleson (Maryknoll, N.Y.: Orbis, 1973).

12. Of course, this does not address the problem of privatization vis-à-vis the *natural* world: to speak of God as active within the social–political sphere does not mean that one can give him an active role within nature or that one looks to one's belief in God to explain events that occur there.

13. See Cardinal Joseph Ratzinger, "Instruction on Certain Aspects of the Theology of Liberation," in Juan Luis Segundo, *Theology and the Church: A Response to Cardinal Ratzinger and a Warning to the Whole Church*, rev. ed., trans. John W. Diercksmeier (San Francisco: Harper and Row, 1987), 173–92.

14. This is not to say that the liberation theologians do not address theodicy in any form. See Gutierrez, *On Job: God-Talk and the Suffering of the Innocent*, trans. Matthew J. O'Connell (Maryknoll, N.Y.: Orbis, 1987).

15. The Greek term *metanoia*, which is used in the New Testament, means literally "change of mind." It is often translated as "conversion." Note Rosemary Radford Ruether's use of the term in her *Sexism and God-Talk: Toward a Feminist Theology* (Boston: Beacon, 1983), 163.

16. Martin Buber, *I and Thou*, trans. Walter Kaufmann (New York: Charles Scribner's Sons, 1970). Buber's position has obviously influenced a large number of feminist religious thinkers. See, e.g., Carol Christ, *Laughter of Aphrodite*, x, 4, 105; Mary Daly, *Beyond God the Father: Toward a Philosophy of Women's Liberation* (Boston: Beacon, 1973), 39; Christine Downing, *The Goddess: Mythological Images of the Feminine* (New York: Crossroad, 1989), 167; Judith Plaskow, *Standing Again at Sinai: Judaism from a Feminist Perspective* (San Francisco: Harper and Row, 1990), 157; Rosemary Radford Ruether, *Gaia and God: An Ecofeminist Theology of Earth Healing* (San Francisco: Harper Collins, 1992), 228, 252, 302 n.36; Dorothee Sölle, *Thinking about God: An Introduction to Theology*, trans. John Bowden (Philadelphia: Trinity Press International, 1990), 185.

17. Feminist suspicion of ontological analysis is understandable, inasmuch as it sometimes proves inimical to the quest for social and political liberation. Sharon Welch charges, for example, that "specific historical concerns are bracketed, and the experience of certain groups of people

is excluded from contributing to or determining that analysis" in the kind of ontology employed in academic theologies. (Sharon D. Welch, *Communities of Resistance and Solidarity: A Feminist Theology of Liberation* [Maryknoll, N.Y.: Orbis, 1985), 38. But these problems more frequently arise with ontologies of human being and the world than with ontologies of God.

18. See Sigmund Freud, *The Future of an Illusion*, ed. and trans. James Strachey (New York: Norton, 1961).

19. See Rebecca S. Chopp, *The Power to Speak: Feminism, Language, God* (New York: Crossroad, 1989).

20. John Dewey, *Reconstruction in Philosophy* (New York: Mentor/New American Library, 1950), 129.

21. William James, *Pragmatism and Four Essays from the Meaning of Truth* (New York: Meridian/New American Library, 1974), 177.

22. See John Dewey, *A Common Faith* (New Haven: Yale, 1934).

23. Ruether, *Sexism and God-Talk*, 69.

24. Ibid., 19.

25. Daly, *Beyond God the Father*, 21.

26. Elisabeth Schüssler Fiorenza, *In Memory of Her: A Feminist Theological Reconstruction of Christian Origins* (New York: Crossroad, 1983), 32–3.

27. Ibid., 32.

28. Plaskow, *Standing Again at Sinai*, 20.

29. Sallie McFague, *Metaphorical Theology: Models of God in Religious Language* (Philadelphia: Fortress Press, 1982), 158. Emphasis added.

30. See above, p. 41 and p. 133, n. 19

31. *Weaving the Visions: New Patterns in Feminist Spirituality*, ed. Judith Plaskow and Carol Christ (San Francisco: Harper and Row, 1989), 93.

32. Chopp, *The Power to Speak*, 83. Chopp is speaking of Karl Barth. Cf. Mary Daly, *Beyond God the Father*, 33.

33. See Nelle Morton, "The Goddess as Metaphoric Image," in *Weaving the Visions*, 111–18.

34. Daly, *Beyond God the Father*, 33. First emphasis is mine.

35. Mary Daly, *Gyn/Ecology: The Metaethics of Radical Feminism* (Boston: Beacon, 1978), 111.

36. Ibid., 49.

37. Carol P. Christ, *Diving Deep and Surfacing: Women Writers on Spiritual Quest* (Boston: Beacon, 1980), 18.

38. Naomi R. Goldenberg, "Archetypal Theory and the Separation of Mind and Body: Reason Enough to Turn to Freud?" in *Weaving the Visions*, 249.

39. Ruether, *Sexism and God-Talk*, 48–49.

40. Ibid., 46.

41. Ibid., 257–58; see also Christ, *Laughter of Aphrodite*, 210, 226; and Carol P. Christ, "Rethinking Theology and Nature," in *Weaving the Visions*, 314, 321, 323.

42. *Weaving the Visions*, 173.

43. Beverly Wildung Harrison, "The Power of Anger in the Work of Love: Christian Ethics for Women and Other Strangers," in *Weaving the Visions*, 225.

44. Sharon D. Welch, *A Feminist Ethic of Risk* (Minneapolis: Fortress, 1990), 173. Welch is responding to Carter Heyward's use of the expression "power of relation" in a way that might be taken to mean that God is not synonymous with the relation but stands behind it as its source. See Carter Heyward, "Sexuality, Love, and Justice," in *Weaving the Visions*, 299. See also Isabel Carter Heyward, *The Redemption of God: A Theology of Mutual Relation* (Lanham, Md.: University Press of America, 1982).

45. Ruether, *Sexism and God-Talk*, 71.

46. Ibid., 163.

47. If one takes the "power of being" in Tillich's sense, then the power of being does deserve to be equated with God, in that Tillich reads the power of being not simply as the force animating nature but as the essential ground of the structure of finite being. Thus, the disrelations

that characterize fallenness can be healed and the meaning of one's being can be fulfilled through the agency of the power of being.

48. Tillich has had an important influence on feminist religious thinkers. There is a natural affinity between the immanent God that Tillich calls the "power of being" and feminist thinking about the divine, even if the specifics of the "power of being" must be reworked for feminist purposes. Note the secondary literature on Tillich's influence on Mary Daly. See, e.g., Mary Ann Stenger, "A Critical Analysis of the Influence of Paul Tillich on Mary Daly's Feminist Theology," *Encounter* 43 (1982): 219–38; Laurel C. Schneider, "From New Being to Meta-Being: A Critical Analysis of Paul Tillich's Influence on Mary Daly," *Soundings* 75 (Summer/ Fall 1992): 421–39; Michel Dion, "Mary Daly, Théologienne et Philosophe Féministe,"*Etudes Theologiques et Religieuses* 4 (1987): 515–34. While the influence of Tillich on feminist religious thought is of course a function of the general contours of his theology, Tillich also seems to have an inkling of some of the specific issues of interest to feminists. As early as 1946, Tillich cites the "patriarchal power of man over woman" as an example of social disruption that needs to be healed (quoted in Donald F. Dreisbach, *Symbols and Salvation: Paul Tillich's Doctrine of Religious Symbols and his Interpretation of the Symbols of the Christian Tradition* [Lanham, Md.: University Press of America, 1993], 99 n.5). And in his *Systematic Theology*, he tells us that the expression "ground of being," which is one of his most often used designations for God, "points to the mother-quality of giving birth, carrying, and embracing, and, at the same time, of calling back, resisting independence of the created, and swallowing it. . . . The attempt to show that nothing can be said about God theologically before the statement is made that he is the power of being in all being [another familiar Tillichian assertion] is, at the same time, a way of reducing the predominance of the male element in the symbolization of the divine." (*Systematic Theology*, 3:293–94.) While there may be as much evidence of male anxiety as of male sensitivity here, and while Tillich's personal life may undermine any apparent feminist sensibilities in his thought, one can at least see points of connection with feminist theology in Tillich's work.

49. Ruether, *Sexism and God-Talk*, 257.

50. "Matrix" is derived from the Latin *matrix*, which is related to *mater*, mother. Ibid., 49.

51. Ruether, *Gaia and God*, 5.

52. See, e.g., Daly, *Beyond God the Father*, 28.

53. Daly, *Gyn/Ecology*, 111.

54. Christ, *Laughter of Aphrodite*, xi.

55. Ibid., 105.

56. Sölle, *Thinking About God*, 181.

57. Kathryn Tanner, *The Politics of God: Christian Theologies and Social Justice* (Minneapolis: Augsburg Fortress, 1992).

58. Indeed, Tanner at one point in her book acknowledges, "my account of God's providential agency provides no clear way of identifying the 'more' that is supposed to be God's contribution. . . ." Ibid., 117.

59. Not all feminist thinkers are enamored of the idea of history, of course. Some hold that feminist consciousness belongs in the timeless world of nature rather than amidst the temporal power struggles that constitute history. But it seems to me that one would miss the importance of feminist nature theologies or thealogies if one failed to recognize that they are already a function of historical struggle: they arise and make sense precisely as responses to a history of sexism and its attendant injustices. Thus the nature Goddess too, in her contemporary incarnation, grapples with historical forces.

60. On the way in which feminist theology has a significant cognitive relation to the world of nature, see below, pp. 111–15.

61. See above, p. 65.

62. See below, pp. 84–85. On the relation of polytheistic and monotheistic elements in concrete feminist spirituality, see Cynthia Eller, *Living in the Lap of the Goddess: The Feminist Spirituality Movement in America* (New York: Crossroad, 1993), 132–35. Eller finds a pattern of "an ultimate monism coupled with an intermediate or functional polytheism." (134)

63. See above, p. 41.

64. See Emmanuel Levinas, *Otherwise than Being or Beyond Essence*, trans. Alphonso Lingis (The Hague: Martinus Nijhoff, 1981). Feminists might well have both good and bad things to say about Levinas: his opposition to all forms of power that quash otherness is surely laudable from a feminist perspective; but his notion that my ethical responsibility to the other puts me in a position of subjection to him or her will likely strike a dissonant chord for feminists.

65. See Martin Heidegger, *Identity and Difference*, trans. Joan Stambaugh (New York: Harper and Row, 1969).

66. "All Lives, All Dances, and All is Loud," in *Technicians of the Sacred*, 2d ed., ed. Jerome Rothenberg (Berkeley: University of California, 1985), 36.

IV. Layers of Continuity and Change

1. Augustine, *Basic Writings of Saint Augustine*, 2 vols., ed. Whitney J. Oates (New York: Random House, 1948), 1:3. Cf. Anselm of Canterbury, "Concerning Truth", in *Truth, Freedom, and Evil: Three Philosophical Dialogues*, ed. and trans. Jasper Hopkins and Herbert Richardson (New York: Harper and Row, 1967), 91–120.

2. Leo Baeck, *The Essence of Judaism* (New York: Schoken, 1948), 142.

3. Frederick J. Streng, *Understanding Religious Life*, third ed. (Belmont, Calif.: Wadsworth, 1985), 2.

4. Freud, *The Future of an Illusion*, 49. Freud's reputation continues to decline, especially in the scientific community. One of the most punishing recent blows was delivered by Frederick Crews in "The Unknown Freud," in *New York Review of Books* 40/19 (November 18, 1993): 55–66. And see the exchange that followed in vol. 41/3 (February 3, 1994): 34–43. Despite such problems, many theologians seem never able to get enough of Freud, a fact indicated by a wide range of contemporary theological works that seriously engage Freudian theory, from Hans Küng's *Freud and the Problem of God*, trans. Edward Quinn (New Haven: Yale, 1979), to Charles Winquist's *Epiphanies of Darkness: Deconstruction in Theology* (Philadelphia: Fortress, 1986). The

continuing theological engagement with Freud can be explained in part by the fact that Freud's notion of the conflicted and deceptive self fits better with traditional Jewish and Christian anthropologies than do merely empirical approaches to selfhood. The Freudian self, even though radically fragmented, or perhaps precisely because it is fragmented, is worthy of theological attention. Furthermore, this fragmented or de-centered Freudian self has a depth and mystery about it that is consistent with religious sensibilities. As Charles Winquist observes, "Criticism and suspicion, introduced especially by Marx, Nietzsche, and Freud, are nihilistic . . . only if one is committed to a construct of subjectivity that values a vision of the world exhausted in reasonableness. But, for many of us, such a rationalization of the world has belittled it, repressed desire, and emptied it of content. A loss of interest and the waning of a sense of importance in experience seem more nihilistic and a greater danger than the drift of subjectivity into ambiguities and indeterminacies. That the world may be more complicated than its Cartesian reconstruction is a relief and a hope. Depth, reality, and importance reside in the complications of experience." *Desiring Theology* (Chicago: University of Chicago, 1995), 21.

5. Deut. 6:4–5; Tillich, *Systematic Theology* 1:11–12.

6. See Edward L. Long, *A Survey of Christian Ethics* (New York: Oxford, 1967), 131.

7. Karl Barth, *The Heidelberg Catechism for Today*, trans. Shirley C. Guthrie, Jr. (Richmond: John Knox, 1964), 29. Emphasis added.

8. This is why one can say, with our definition of God, that God ultimately informs the believer's every thought and action.

9. The famous passage in 1 John according to which "whoever does not love does not know God; for God is love," intends the former pattern, I think—devotion to God automatically results in the proper relation to all other things (including human beings)—but it can be read in terms of the enactment pattern—devotion to God *is* proper relation to all other things. See 1 John 4:8, NRSV.

10. In the case of Tillich's own theology, the situation is ambiguous: something like the artifact relation between God and human being remains, but it is filtered through the idealist elements of Tillich's ontology.

11. Experience, for Kant, is "knowledge by means of connected percep-
    tions" (Immanuel Kant, *Critique of Pure Reason*, trans. Norman Kemp
    Smith [New York: St. Martin's, 1965], 171). "Perception" is explained
    this way: "What is first *given* to us is appearance. When combined with
    consciousness, it is called perception" (Ibid., 143; emphasis added).
    And note that "*intuition* takes place only so far as the object is *given* to
    us" (Ibid., 65; emphasis added).

12. William James, *The Varieties of Religious Experience* (New York: Mentor-
    New American Library, 1958), 61. Emphasis in text.

13. One might counter that I can directly experience nature as a whole
    through something like the so-called oceanic feeling. But this is not as
    direct as it seems, for I interpret that feeling as an experience of oneness
    with nature, as opposed to an experience of something else, usually
    because I have the feeling while walking through the woods, looking at
    the sea, and so on. These particular woods or this particular portion of
    the sea provide a concrete content of consciousness that stands in for
    the whole of nature: in the language I employ below, these parts of
    nature are "symbols" of the whole. Thus our experience of the whole of
    nature here is mediated through symbols.

14. See above, p. 63.

15. Gadamer, *Truth and Method*, 136.

16. Cf. Emile Durkheim's claim that symbols are needed to make the social
    whole graspable for the primitive mind. As Evans-Pritchard explains
    Durkheim's position, quoting Durkheim in the process, "Concrete
    symbols are necessary because 'the clan is too complex a reality to be
    represented clearly in all its complex unity by such rudimentary intelli-
    gences.' Unsophisticated minds cannot think of themselves as a social
    group except through material symbols" (E.E. Evans-Pritchard,
    Theories of Primitive Religion [London: Oxford, 1965], 59). Durkheim's
    one error here, I think, is to assume that symbols are required for this
    purpose only by "rudimentary intelligences."

17. Despite the power of symbolic presence, there is a modesty attached to
    the reception of this symbolic presence, a modesty that does not char-
    acterize the way in which ordinary, nonsymbolic thinking makes things
    present. Ordinary thinking tempts me with the illusion of *pure*

presence. I attempt to master what I am thinking about, to force it in its entirety and in its very essence into the "now" of consciousness. But the symbol promises no such pure presence. It is by its very nature simultaneously affirmation and negation. That is, the symbol both is what it symbolizes—i.e., figuratively—and is not what it symbolizes— i.e., literally. (See Tillich, *Systematic Theology* 1:239: "a symbolic expression is one whose proper meaning is negated by that to which it points. And yet it is also affirmed by it, and this affirmation gives the symbolic expression an adequate basis for pointing beyond itself." Cf. McFague, *Models of God*, 33–34.) Thus, symbolic presence should escape the strictures against the illusion of pure presence that are articulated in contemporary post-structuralist thought.

18. This is what Tillich has in mind when he talks about symbols "participating" in what they symbolize. I attempt a detailed clarification of Tillich's use of the notion of participation in my *Symbol and Empowerment*, 33–41. Note that, before Tillich, Coleridge had already claimed that a symbol "always partakes of the Reality which it renders intelligible." See *The Collected Works of Samuel Taylor Coleridge*, vol. 6, ed. R. J. White (Princeton: Princeton University Press, 1972), 30.

19. See Luke 15:8–10.

20. One of the reasons imaginary givenness is sufficient for religious experience in enactment piety is that enactment piety does not need to use religious experience as an epistemological defense; an enactment theology does not claim that God or Goddess is a being existing independently of the persons who are in relation to God or Goddess.

21. Even traditional theism's concept of God as a personal supreme being could be used as a *symbol* of the enacted God. In this case, the enacted God might be regarded as an instance of what Tillich calls "the God beyond God": the traditional notion of God loses its literal referential function and serves as a symbol pointing beyond itself to a deity understood as somehow more ultimate than a supernatural being. Cf. Paul Tillich, *The Courage to Be* (New Haven: Yale, 1952), 186–90. In addition, for a specifically Christian enactment theology, the need for a symbol to make God present may point to the revelatory role of the Christ, i.e., to the Christ as the central symbol through which God is

revealed. Whether any of these symbols is fully *experiential* depends on the material that constitutes it.

22. See p. 41 above.

23. Robert P. Scharlemann, "The Being of God When God Is Not Being God," in *Deconstruction and Theology*, Thomas J.J. Altizer, et al. (New York: Crossroad, 1982), 81.

24. Postmodernist consciousness in particular attacks these currents. But feminism, as a liberatory movement, stands in an ambiguous relation to postmodernism. See, e.g., Sabina Lovibond, "Feminism and Postmodernism," in *New Left Review* 178 (November–December 1989): 5–28.

25. Cf. Kathryn Tanner's charge that, in some radically revisionist theologies, "the theological acccount seems to be just a redescription of a social agenda to include another personal agent, God, or to encompass a cosmic dimension." *The Politics of God*, 256.

26. Isa. 1:11, 13, 17. NRSV.

27. See, for example, chaps. 5 and 6 in Eller, *Living in the Lap of the Goddess*.

28. *Systematic Theology* 1:14.

29. See Tillich, *The Courage to Be*, 32–63.

30. This is an instance where the exigencies of the enactment model, as well as the particular convictions of thinkers such as Ruether and Christ, lead us in a different direction from concrete feminist spirituality, which tends to embrace the idea of reincarnation.

31. See Ruether, *Sexism and God-Talk*, 163.

32. Intriguing insights on these matters are offered in Josiah Royce's largely neglected later work. Royce too thinks of the divine in terms of a relation. More specifically, he describes an infinite community of interpretation. Royce's proposal must be acknowledge to be out of step with contemporary philosophical sensibilities. His version of the overarching relation that is divinity and, in fact, reality as a whole, has quite different ontological implications from the relation that I have taken to be the heart of enactment theology. Royce himself sees his proposal as a

"form of metaphysical idealism," albeit "a somewhat new form" (Josiah Royce, *The Problem of Christianity* [Chicago:University of Chicago, 1968; originally published 1918], 38; 51). But his attention to the ideas of community as the essence of the divine, the possibility of sin in the form of disloyalty to this universal community, and how atonement can be effected to overcome this sin, provides clues that practitioners of an enactment theology might usefully follow up in their attempt to work out their responses to moral anxiety.

33. See Geertz, "Religion as a Cultural System," 90, 98–108.

34. In other words, we have taken largely at face value both the explicit claims of the feminist theologies that we have treated, and the implicit claims that I have suggested follow from the notion of an enactment religiosity.

V. The Future of God

1. The situation is analogous to the so-called three body problem in Newtonian physics: if there is just one planet orbiting a sun, we can calculate the planet's path using a fairly simply formula. But if we complicate the gravitational interactions by adding a third body, we shall be forced to engage in laborious calculations in order to describe what happens. And if one were to attempt to map out the interaction of a large number of bodies, such as the molecules in a gas, one would discover that the task is simply impossible. See Richard P. Feynman, Robert B.Leighton, and Matthew Sands, *The Feynman Lectures on Physics* (Reading, Mass: Addison-Wesley, 1963), I–10–1.

2. Bloom, *The American Religion*, 257.

3. While West focuses more directly upon religion in some of his other works, he has much to say about the effects of capitalism on minority communities in his more recent and popular book, *Race Matters* (Boston: Beacon, 1993). See also Cornel West, "The 1994 Inaugural Aims of Religion Address," *Criterion* 33/2 (Spring/Summer, 1994): 16–25.

4. It may be possible, of course, that the continuing expansion of electronic communications media, from special-interest cable television

channels to computer networks, will result in electronic communities. We may now have to look for communities and institutions at points in the social structure where they could not have existed before. Perhaps an enactment piety, especially of the feminist variety, could establish a base of this sort.

5. It is important to remember, though, that this traditional idea was not itself monolithic; the idea of God has changed continually throughout its history.

6. Rahner, *Foundations of Christian Faith*, 48.

7. Ibid., 49.

8. Ibid., 48.

9. See Martin Heidegger, *Being and Time*, trans. John Macquarrie and Edward Robinson (New York: Harper and Row, 1962), 279–311.

10. Kant, *Critique of Pure Reason*, 308–570.

11. For a clear analysis of Kierkegaard's notion of the task of becoming a self, see John W. Elrod, *Being and Existence in Kierkegaard's Pseudonymous Works* (Princeton: Princeton University Press, 1975).

12. There may be other notions of an ultimate horizon in addition to the Western notion of God that can accomplish the same thing as the idea of God here. Note, however, that probably not just any conception of an ultimate or infinite horizon will do. The Buddhist concept of nirvana, for example, can hardly be expected to encourage the construction of selfhood, given its focus precisely on the extinction of self.

13. Indeed, consider how the concept of God has sometimes functioned for the atheist in the modern West as a negative impetus to securing a potent sense of selfhood. The Nietzschean atheist, for example, protests against the idea of God as something that undermines the self's autonomy and dignity.

14. Cf. Peter L. Berger and Thomas Luckmann, *The Social Construction of Reality: A Treatise in the Sociology of Knowledge* (Garden City, N.Y.: Doubleday-Anchor, 1966), 47–52.

15. In Mary Daly's vision of woman, for instance, centeredness is crucial: "Unlike the suspended, crucified, self-sacrificing victim, she stands

stably on the earth, Self-assuring and Self-centering" (*Gyn/Ecology*, 388). Daly celebrates "Self-centering Spinsters" who move about the axis of their own be-ing (ibid., 391). And Ruether calls us to "affirm the integrity of our personal center of being, in mutuality with the personal centers of all other beings across species and, at the same time, accept the transience of these personal selves" (*Gaia and God*, 251).

16. Quoted in Elizabeth Grosz, *Sexual Subversions: Three French Feminists* (Sydney: Allen and Unwin, 1989), 153.

17. Ibid.

18. This may be only a "tacit" capability, in Michael Polanyi's sense of the term; it need not be thematic or capable of theoretical articulation. See Michael Polanyi, *Personal Knowledge: Towards a Post-Critical Philosophy* (Chicago: Univeristy of Chicago, 1962).

19. Probably the most important use of the concept of *krisis* in modern theology is found in Karl Barth's *Epistle to the Romans*, trans. Edwyn C. Hoskyns (London: Oxford, 1968), 10.

20. Baeck, *The Essence of Judaism*, 84

21. See above, p. 71.

22. Ruether, *Gaia and God*, 194–95.

23. See above, pp. 94-95.

24. For the notion of a fictive religiosity, see Lonnie D. Kliever, "Fictive Religion: Rhetoric and Play," *Journal of the American Academy of Religion* 49 (1981): 657–69.

25. See Hans Vaihinger, *The Philosophy of As If: A System of the Theoretical, Practical and Religious Fictions of Mankind*, 2d ed., trans. C. K. Ogden (New York: Harcourt, 1935).

26. Given that feminist religious thought has served as our point of departure for discussing enactment theology, it is worthwhile to note that there has been a tendency among some feminist thinkers to reject as oppressive and patriarchal the kind of investment in reason presupposed by this intellectual, cognitive component of theology. But other feminist thinkers have begun to speak out against the dangers to feminism in the denigration of reason and against the faulty assumptions

upon which any such denigration rests. See, e.g., Martha Nussbaum, "Feminists and Philosophy," *New York Review of Books* 41/17 (October 20, 1994): 59–63.

Epilogue

1. The phrase, "morally exhuasted" is used by Tom Morganthau in his discussion of the demagogic treatment of IQ, class, and race by Charles Murray and Richard Herrnstein in their book, *The Bell Curve: Intelligence and Class Structure in American Life* (New York: Free Press, 1994). See "IQ: Is It Destiny?" *Newsweek*, October 24, 1994, 53.

2. See Welch, *A Feminist Ethic of Risk.*

3. The assertion that "theology is anthropology" was penned by Ludwig Feuerbach, in which instance it had a decidedly reductionistic meaning. See his *The Essence of Christianity*, trans. George Eliot (New York: Harper and Row, 1957), xxxvii.

4. See above, p. 63.

5. Elie Wiesel, from an interview in the film, *Judaism: The Chosen People*, vol. 7 of *The Long Search*, conceived and narrated Ronald Eyre, produced Peter Montagnon, directed Brian Lewis (New York: Time-Life Video, 1977).

Index

Of Related Interest from Continuum

Carol P. Christ

Odyssey with the Goddess: A Spiritual Quest in Crete

A personal spiritual journey and thealogy by the acclaimed author of *Laughter of Aphrodite* and other best-selling books.

"Luminous prose. . . . Christ's chronicle is a welcome addition to collections in women's spirituality. Highly recommended." —*Library Journal*

192 pages 0–8264–0793–5 $18.95 hardcover

John Fenwick and Bryan Spinks

Worship in Transition: The Liturgical Movement in the Twentieth Century

This much-needed study defines and explains the many changes in liturgy and worship that have swept Christian churches in the twentieth century.

"Very clear, readable, and comprehensive."—Paul F. Bradshaw

216 pages 0–8264–0827–3 $17.95 paperback

Patricia Reis

Daughters of Saturn: From Father's Daughter to Creative Woman

A compelling examination of the father–daughter relationship, particularly in its archetypal dimensions with respect to fathers' impact on daughters' creative lives.

"A brilliant analysis. . . . A unique model for the feminine creative process." —Linda Leonard

288 pages 0–8264–0812–5 $24.95 hardcover

Patricia Reis

Through the Goddess: A Woman's Way of Healing

The in-dwelling Goddess is shown to be a much-needed source for spiritual, psychological, and physical healing.

"This wise and gentle book is a healing work."—Charlene Spretnak

240 pages 0–8264–0856–7 $14.95 paperback.

Elisabeth Schüssler Fiorenza

Jesus: Miriam's Child, Sophia's Prophet—Critical Issues in Feminist Christology

"No Christology today will be adequate that does not take seriously Schüssler Fiorenza's unsettling challenge to assess critically how social and political forces have shaped Christian doctrine and how these doctrines impact the lives of women and others."—*Commonweal*

"This work is . . . at the heart of cutting-edge critical political and theological debate."—*Library Journal*

272 pages 0–8264–8358–3 $16.95 paperback

Ita Sheres and Anne Kohn Blau

The Truth about the Virgin: Sex and Ritual in the Dead Sea Scrolls

Unlocks some of the deepest secrets of the Dead Sea Scrolls: how at Qumram, a select group of virgin females were pledged in an immaculate conception ceremony reminiscent of the ancient Goddess religion.

"This pioneering work is not for the fainthearted but will light the way for intrepid searchers for the truth."—David Noel Freedman

252 pages 0–8264–0816–8 $27.50 hardcover

Available at your bookstore or from the publisher: **The Continuum Publishing Company, 370 Lexington Avenue, New York, NY 10017 1–800–937–5557**